281.9 H434
Healing : Orthodox Christian
perspectives in medicine,
psychology, and religion

281.9
H434

A Publication of
THE ORTHODOX CHRISTIAN ASSOCIATION OF
MEDICINE, PSYCHOLOGY, AND RELIGION

HEALING

Orthodox Christian Perspectives in
Medicine, Psychology, and Religion

Edited by
John T. Chirban

HOLY CROSS ORTHODOX PRESS
Brookline, Massachusetts 02146

050308

© Copyright 1991 by Holy Cross Orthodox Press

Published by Holy Cross Orthodox Press
50 Goddard Avenue
Brookline, Massachusetts 02146

All rights reserved

Library of Congress Cataloging-in-Publication Data

Healing: Orthodox Christian perspectives in medicine, psychology, and religion:edited by John T. Chirban.
p. / cm.
At head of title: The Orthodox Christian Association of Medicine, Psychology, and Religion.
"Papers delivered at the first national conference of the Orthodox Christian Association of Medicine, Psychology, and Religion" — Foreword.
ISBN 0-917651-84-7
1. Medicine — Religious aspects — Orthodox Eastern Church — Congresses. 2. Mental health — Religious aspects — Orthodox Eastern — Doctrines — Congresses.
I. Chirban, John T.
II. Orthodox Christian Association of Medicine, Psychology and Religion.

BX323.H38   1991   91-6678
261.561 — dc20   CIP

For Those Who Heal
And For Those Who Are Healed

"The Kingdom of Heaven is at hand; heal the sick, raise the dead, cleanse the lepers, cast out demons."

Matthew 10.7-8

CONTENTS

Foreword	ix
Preface	xi

PART ONE: KEYNOTE ADDRESS

Healing: The Power of Medicine, Psychology, and Religion JOHN T. CHIRBAN	1

PART TWO: DEPRESSION

Introduction THEODORE BILILIES	9
Depression: Medical Perspective JOHN DEMAKIS	11
Depression: Psychological Perspective NICHOLAS D. KOKONIS	17
Depression: Religious Perspective NICHOLAS KROMMYDAS	23

PART THREE: GENETIC ENGINEERING. WHERE DO WE DRAW THE LINE?

Introduction PAUL TALAGAN	27
Genetic Engineering: Scientific Perspective PETER H. DIAMANDIS	29
Genetic Engineering: Religious Perspective JOHN BRECK	37

PART FOUR: MIRACLES. SCIENTIFIC AND RELIGIOUS REFLECTIONS

Introduction
GREGORY PHELAN   43

Miracles: Scientific Reflections
THEOHARIS C. THEOHARIDES   45

Miracles: Religious Reflections
JOHN MEYENDORFF   51

PART FIVE: AIDS: ACQUIRED IMMUNE DEFICIENCY SYNDROME

Introduction
ANTHONY VASILAS   57

Human Immunodeficiency Virus (HIV) Infections and Acquired Immunodeficiency Syndrome (AIDS): Impacts on Lifestyles in the 21st Century
GEORGE J. PAZIN   59

Psycho-social and Theological Concerns Related to the Care of Persons with AIDS
PETER POULOS   65

AIDS: Moral Crisis?
MILTON B. EFTHIMIOU   73

The OCAMPR Report on AIDS
FORUM ON AIDS   78

Contributors   83

Foreword

HEALING: ORTHODOX CHRISTIAN PERSPECTIVES IN MEDICINE, Psychology, and Religion is a volume of timely papers concerning subjects of central importance for the Church. I take special pleasure in endorsing this book, not only because of the highly significant articles about our faith and the sciences, but also because of what this book represents for Orthodoxy in America.

This volume presents papers delivered at the first national conference of the Orthodox Christian Association of Medicine, Psychology and Religion. It inaugurates a new and important effort of our Orthodox Church in the Americas by bringing our medical, psychological, and religious leaders together to share and to learn and to address issues of critical concern of our people. I take delight in this effort which is committed to sharing the light of our Lord and Savior Jesus Christ and pray that the O.C.A.M.P.R. prospers in sharing "all that is good."

Bishop Methodios
Brookline, Massachusetts

Preface

AS HUMAN BEINGS ARE UNDERSTOOD AS A COMPLICATED INteraction of body, mind, and soul, efforts to heal the person, particularly in modern times, suffer by compartmentalization in the disciplines of medicine, psychology, and religion. Although each of these disciplines more or less dovetails and affects the other, it is not uncommon that these efforts are independent, if not adversarial, of one another in practice.

In contrast to this trend, Orthodox Christian anthropology teaches that the human being is a psychosomatic whole and emphasizes the importance of synergy and interdependence in the healing disciplines. The Orthodox Christian Association of Medicine, Psychology, and Religion (O.C.A.M.P.R.) has been developed in the service of this principle. This volume includes papers presented by Orthodox Christian physicians, psychologists, and religious leaders of the founding conference of this association.

These papers, as well as the effort in general, work to cultivate a holistic perspective concerning one's growth in Christ. These papers, which address the theme of healing from an Orthodox Christian perspective, focus on subjects that may be perceived as appropriate to specific disciplines yet demonstrate the role of other disciplines (e.g. medicine — AIDS or Genetic Engineering; psychology — depression; and religion — miracles). All present interdisciplinary resourcefulness.

The goals of the O.C.A.M.P.R. are to facilitate Christian fellowship in medicine, psychology, and religion; interdisciplinary dialogue; integration of the assumptions of medicine, psychology, and religion; education of interdisciplinary studies and the Orthodox faith; and application of services for the community. As a "new discipline," by definition of the goals of O.C.A.M.P.R., this volume is the first step toward the difficult but essential objectives.

The papers offered here bring together not only members of various disciplines, but also individuals from various jurisdictions toward the unifying goal of understanding both the needs and the nature of the human person and healing.

In the Keynote Address, I speak about the importance of interdisciplinary cooperation to support total health for human life. I review the advances in each of these disciplines and explains how Orthodox Christian theology may guide a unified expression for health care.

Drs. John Demakis, Nicholas Kokonis, and Rev. Nicholas Krommydas provide insightful information about how depression can be treated from their respective disciplines and, specifically, how they understand that their professional training would come to bear support in the case study of an elderly man who is suffering from clinical depression.

Dr. Peter Diamandis and Rev. Dr. John Breck examine the ethical dilemma brought on by advances in genetic engineering. From scientific and theological perspectives, both papers emphasize the necessity of sound ethical judgments for genetic engineering and explain how theology may guide such thought.

Miracles serve as the subject for examination from scientific and religious perspectives by Dr. Theoharis Theoharides and Rev. Dr. John Meyendorff, respectively. After clarifying the understanding of miracles from scientific and religious perspectives, both speakers identify the boundaries of religion and medicine, as well as their faithful position that God works beyond human epistomology.

The subject on Acquired Immune Deficiency Syndrome (AIDS) provides challenges for Orthodox Christian physicians, psychologists, and religious leaders. Dr. George Pazin places our medical understanding of AIDS in perspective of the proper behavior patterns necessary to avoid contracting HIV infection. Rev. Milton Efthimiou calls for a personal "Christian response" to the persons suffering from AIDS, while Peter Poulos speaks about health professionals need to sensitize themselves in order to heal those afflicted by Human-Immunodeficiency Virus (HIV). In response to a charge from this conference, "The O.C.A.M.P.R. Report on AIDS" brings together leaders in the various disciplines to provide answers to four basic questions about AIDS;

1. Should there be a change in the administration of Holy Communion to guard against the possible contamination or to respond to the fear of HIV?

2. Should people wanting to marry be tested for HIV?

3. What kind of behavior should be recommended in order to avoid the spread of AIDS?

4. How do we counsel people to respond to AIDS patients and to the fear of the spread of this disease?

John Chirban
Lexington, Massachusetts

PART ONE
KEYNOTE ADDRESS

Healing: The Power of Medicine, Psychology, and Religion

JOHN T. CHIRBAN

I WOULD LIKE TO BEGIN BY CHARACTERIZING HISTORICALLY the quality of interaction between medicine, psychology, and religion and then to identify some of the challenges raised by the theme, "Healing," and by our new organization — The Orthodox Christian Association of Medicine, Psychology, and Religion (O.C.A.M.P.R.).

The work of Jesus Christ to a great extent is an account of healing: restoring, curing, making whole. For most of us in this room, who busy ourselves with the particular aspects of our disciplines, it is the experience of participating or assisting in the healing process that gives our lives meaning. Through participation in what is the creative art of healing, we witness the *power* of the life force — and facilitate the action of healthful growth of body, mind, and soul.

"Healing" is an *active* verb, describing tremendous positive possibilities, and it is the *single greatest* challenge for most of us. It assists rightness, wholeness, and soundness. And although it may be true that the areas of medicine, psychology, and religion rarely share mutual understanding, this word is respected in each of these domains as a *valid* goal and as an ultimate purpose. What we wish to recognize in an organization such as the O.C.A.M.P.R. is that our notions of healing may well be limited by the foci and parameters of our particular disciplines, and if we wish to heal a person significantly, we need a shared vision of whole being.

As Christians, we recognize that Christ's healing was founded squarely on the Hebraic holistic view of man — a tradition valued and preserved by the Church Fathers. Our culture seems to be influenced more by the Greek ideas of dualism (or dividing the human being) and rationalism (seeing the human as merely thinking — not feeling), which flourished during the period of the scholastics and which has so saturated modern studies and society.

In this way, our approach to "healing" has become fragmented. A tension can be witnessed between the existential, holistic concrete early Hebrew and Christian emphasis concerning the human person, and the Greek idealistic, dualistic, and rationalistic approaches of the person which the disciplines of medicine, psychology, and religion illustrate today.

On the one hand, we wish to acknowledge the valuable contributions resulting from the focused, independent studies of these fields; on the other hand, we recognize that professionals for quite some time have become isolated and parochial and feel so confident in their private corners of investigations, that many believe that the fullness of life and the entire world could be viewed from their particular looking glass.

As for those being healed, the patients and the parishioners, for example, few of our people have usually been converted in total to becoming exclusive devotees of such approaches, which would seem to suggest that each approach, in and of itself, does not fulfill the individual. *Nevertheless, we, in effect, have divided our services.* So most individuals have to orchestrate their plans of how to meet the whole range of their physical, psychological, and spiritual needs. As a result, our culture is a potpourri of approaches, parts, and choices of which the people finally ask: "Where is it all leading?" "Can anyone really understand me?"

In the face of a pluralistic society which affirms all things and usually commits itself to none, we must not be surprised, therefore, but rather attempt to understand and to empathize with the individual who experiences the results and eventual symptoms of this lack of direction and disharmony of body, mind, and soul in modern society: whether it be through the signs of the suicidal teenager, the programming of Mooneys, or terminal illness itself.

Ever since Hippocreates, especially in the last five centuries, a division has taken place that relegates the care of man's physical well-being to the medical profession and the care of man's spiritual being to the Church realm. The denial of the supernatural origin of disease seems to have accelerated the progress of the medical sciences and created the subsequent high esteem in which they are held today. While medicine has increasingly gained in importance — to the point of possessing a monopoly of the authority to heal the physical being — the Church's philosophy of healing the whole person has decreased in importance and its healing role eventually has been limited to the spiritual dimension. To a large extent, modern-day disciplines, such as medicine, psychology, and religion, germinated during the period of the scholastics. A tension has been created between the approach of these disciplines to healing and the Patristic approach.

Clearly, this fragmented approach to understanding man and addressing his needs has resulted in valuable contributions from these disciplines. However, this climate has left "healers" isolated and parochial at one extreme feeling overly confident of the healing powers they have derived from their investigation, which they might perceive as the fullness of life, to the other extreme of being fearful that their perceptions may be invalidated by the professional criteria of other disciplines.

In reality, the strict following of only one method of healing is rarely comprehensive and is hardly ever practiced. Few Orthodox people are converts to the notion that they should become devotees of only one approach to healing. For example, some have dilemma of who to call when not feeling well: a priest for prayer or exorcism; a psychologist for an antidepressant or psychotherapy; or a physician to identify a physical cause for the ailment.

Because of this fragmented approach to health, Orthodox people are seldom clear about how to be healed or, for that matter, what constitutes good health. The offer of a potpourri of approaches and choices leads one to ask, "Does anyone really understand my pain and my needs?"

Furthermore, inconsistencies and ambiguities often exist in what is said and what is done. For example, one may be told to have faith in order to be healthy and yet be treated with scientific intervention when not feeling well with little clarity about how such decisions are made. What health care and spiritual providers are saying and what they are doing seem in such instances to be at odds.

Interestingly enough, in spite of these trends, what we are observing today is that each of our disciplines has for the most part been a law unto itself. Independent study has led each to investigate what the others have to offer:

> *In Medicine*: Medical schools are now establishing departments of behavioral medicines (in effect, psychology), and physicians are leading research on the value of meditation (in effect,

religion) on the immunological, cardiovascular, and gastrointestinal systems as well as the body in general.

In Psychology: Psychologists are spearheading studies in psychoneuroimmunology and neuropsychology (in effect, medicine), while examining the component of "love" (in effect, religion) as essential for emotional stability.

In Religion: Theologians and clergy who have reflected — though often theoretically — on the psychosomatic nature of a person (in effect, the concerns of medicine and religion) are realizing how essential clinical, direct applications are for their *words* with regard to the healing process and the action of healing itself.

It seems that we come full circle. And if this is the fortunate case — and once more we will see the human person as he or she truly is, as whole — how shall *we* approach our healing? Are we prepared to heal the whole person?

Will we continue only to be technicians of our particular expertise? Or do we wish to ask how our God-blessed talents can fit into the vision of the whole man and whole woman?

Today, a quiet revolution is evolving in the areas of healing and health. Often called "holistic" medicine (which, because of its diffuse definition, for some carries a pejorative connotation), the thrust of this movement treats the person as a unity of body, mind, and spirit. Illness, then, is looked upon as multidimensional; holistic medicine considers the close connection between a person's sense of well-being, or lack of it, and health. Its focus includes the biology of the individual, the effects of external stress on the individual, and the loss of spiritual orientation within. In short, one's total being is considered when considering illness, healing, and growth.

The research to support this direction of investigation, even by conservative evaluation, is inviting. In a recent report, the Center for Disease Control has documented that *lifestyle* is *nearly 300%* more a factor in the cause of death than is human biology. The report also implicates the *environment* over human biology as the *cause* of terminal illness.

In the medical community, a holistic approach to healing begins to replace a mechanical, or entirely biochemical, paradigm of the person. Where before, only as a last resort, would medicine call upon the so-called "ancilliary services" of psychology and religion, now the three fields begin to work in concert.

In the psychological community, psychologists begin to release healing from the limitations of animalistic and mechanical assumptions which they have previously employed to explain human behavior. Psychology has new mandates for both health psychology and transpersonal psychology.

In the religious community, the Church begins to free healing from the bonds of mere educational and ritualistic orientations, where before, it only *spoke* of what was *said*, and it is now a force of action and an expression which is the essence of the encounter with God.

With this interdisciplinary trend, the ground seems fertile for our work: it is now time to *ask*, to *wonder*, to *discover*, to *explore* how the Orthodox may bring their talent and their faith to the healing process; to be whole themselves and to serve as vehicles for healing in modern times.

Richard R. Niebuhr, in his book *Experiencing Religion*, states, "Many explain that modern man cannot believe in miracles; it isn't that modern man cannot believe in miracles, it's just that he needs to be shown how."

And so it is with us. Enough has been *said* by physicians and psychologists who advocate the necessity for whole health or by theologians who proclaim that we must approach a neo-patristic synthesis. Rather than setting the table once more with regard to what should be done, let us, with God's grace, endeavor to bring together the *fascinating* power and range of energies with which we have been endowed to heal.

Our epistemology, our approach to truth, as Orthodox, affirms knowledge as a spiritual activity of inner illumination — finding no dichotomy between reason and spiritual reality. At the same time, our tradition is opposed both to idealism and spiritualism, as well as empiricism — because these approaches are cut off by their own definitions, locked in the realms of ideas or matter, respectively.

Interestingly, the Fathers of the Church emphasized the positive value of reason, stating that it may lead to "true knowing," a state toward which our disciplines seem to move today. Knowledge for the *Fathers*, however, is more than intellectual: it is moral, affective, experiential, ontological and in agreement with nature. These qualities are aspects of a full life.

Through our particular educations, we, the so-called miracle workers of medicine, psychology, and religion, have been affected by the systems of thought that are actually foreign to our faith and its interest in the whole person. Whether this be through the scientific method of the hard sciences, the philosophical assumptions underpinning psychological theories or the scholasticism implanted in the structure of our theological schools, our approaches and the direction of healing in general mainfest a lack of spiritual focus.

And although we may theoretically discuss the implications of how this affects the way we live our lives, personally, it also affects how we care for and "heal" others:

For the doctor, when the test results of a patient reveals lung cancer, what do you do?

For the psychologist, when a patient says, "I've had surgery, a year of chemo and endless tests. I'm tired of it. I'd rather die than go through all this. I'm saying — no more!", what do you say?

For the clergyman, when a mother learns that her four-year old has leukemia and exclaims, "Why does God punish people? Timmy's so good. Father, it's not fair." What should occur?

Should each of these professionals turn to their traditional treatment plan alone? Can they call upon others? Do they play God? Or should they call upon God — as did Jesus and Peter — and ask for a miracle before them. Can we envision God actually working through us — not on our terms alone but with Him?

I will digress a moment to tell you a personal story. About five years ago my mother had a cyst on her breast that was diagnosed as a benign growth by three different physicians. Upon pre-surgical examination, a young surgeon shared his thoughts that the growth was indeed malignant. A tide of fear changed my mother's disposition.

When I called the next day and I learned how frightened she was, I decided to leave Boston and go to see her in Chicago.

When I arrived at the Columbus Hospital I found my mother very calm and natural.

I was surprised and asked what had happened. I learned that after I telephoned, the same young surgeon who had come the day before and offered the prognosis of cancer had come again, and, now, seeing my mother's distress, prayed with her, literally holding her hand, for *one* hour, calling upon God to disolve the cancer. He prayed with my sister and with the woman who was in the adjoining room — with such power and sincerity all of them felt changed.

As it turned out, my mother did have a malignancy and the young surgeon, who has since become a close friend, shared with me that he was sorry that a radical miracle had not occurred as he had prayed. I was very moved by his faith but felt that truly a miracle had occurred. For he had given my mother the direction in God to live to this day with a metastatic illness which we were told would kill her within two years.

In the O.C.A.M.P.R., we are called to a creative, a difficult, and immensely important and fulfilling task. The issue for us is not the question of a need for integration, but moreover how to coordinate the efforts of our individual specialized approaches and our faith for the good of those whom we serve. We may concur with one another on the need for a holistic approach in healing. We may acknowledge a fundamental agreement with respect to the principle underlying our faith and its confirmation by scientific measures. But to expect a fundamental change, we must work at all levels — fellowship, clinics, services, missions.

"Holistic" health often conjures up "far out" approaches toward cure; in these, we are clearly not interested. What we seek are solid methods within our disciplines based upon the commitment of faith.

The method to achieve these ends could begin with an affirmation of the love of God which all of us share. Our Lord tells us, "The truth will set you free." To experience life as freedom is to accept many ways of knowing. For the truth of God, by definition, can never conflict with the universe that he created, but can only render us whole.

We need to constantly affirm humbly the presence of God amongst us, the value of his creation in each of us, and an awareness to the fact of our paradoxically small yet infinitely great potential; to ask some serious questions about our personal faith; to work out the details of our faith and professional lives; to ponder the concrete problems of our day; and to offer our best efforts toward constructive results.

In the initial months of this organization, we have received numerous letters from Orthodox concerned about health and faith — the interest has been impressive and in every instance positive. We must nurture this interest to unite, to bring our people together from their various disciplines, nurture their decision to serve, and embrace them as brothers and sisters in a cause.

Our inter-Orthodox initiative also provides an excellent opportunity to gather together with Orthodox Christians of various jurisdictions, not only around the secondary matters socializing and ethnic concerns, but around the real work of our faith. It may well be as Patriarch Athenagoras suggested in his words about ecumenism: That the Orthodox may achieve union first through love and works, and then through theological decree.

Our mission provides a forum to understand and to serve better our fellow man. But much more importantly, this conference inaugurates a turning point for our theology and our Church in America: Unity of churches; unity of the person; and unity of theory and application.

I pray that our Lord Jesus Christ is in our hearts and perceived through our eyes as we begin.

PART TWO
DEPRESSION

Introduction

THEODORE BILILIES

OUR THEME IS HEALING. BY HEALING, WE MEAN TO CONNOTE a creative process which works towards the unity of body, mind, and soul. It is more than physical health, psychological harmony, or spiritual well-being. It is a holistic synthesis of the best of all three of our disciplines. It is the acknowledgement that the whole is more than just the sum of the parts; it is a recognition of the fundamental fact that we cannot hope to heal or be healed alone; that we need each other to heal each other, and to heal ourselves. We need each other because no one alone, nor any one discipline, can effect complete healing; that is, the restoration of the fully human person. Although cures exist, we are brought together here today by our acknowledgement, tacitly or openly, that we need each other, and that we need to learn what each other has to offer.

We, even more fundamentally than this, are brought together today by our personal as well as professional commitment to serve Jesus Christ. It is in this spirit and from this perspective of synthesis and mutuality that I introduce the speakers and our task.

Now for a moment, I thought I might sound like a boxing referee in introducing our task this afternoon: "In this corner, medicine, in this corner, psychology. . . !" That is precisely what we seek to avoid. We will all view a videotape of a man in need of healing and ask our kind participants to render their thoughts and the approaches they would use in healing this individual. This exercise, hopefully, will demonstrate to all of us how compatible many of our concerns and commitments are, and yet how distinct and different we are. Finally, we might consider the idea that there are many paths to healing, and that we might find that traveling several of the paths together takes us to our destination faster and with greater assurance.

Depression: Medical Perspective

JOHN DEMAKIS

CASE PRESENTATION

History: The patient is an eighty-year-old white male with significant arthritis. His wife, who had been his main support, died thirteen months ago. The patient had been doing well until one month ago when on the anniversary of his wife's death, he attempted suicide.

The patient now lives alone in a trailer. He has a daughter who helps him, but she has other responsibilities as well. The patient states he does not want to be dependent on his daughter. The patient also states that he is disgusted with himself. He doesn't think he will ever get well but will always be a "cripple."

Physical: The patient appears to be an elderly white male in a wheelchair who is alert and responsive. He appears mildly agitated with episodes of crying and wringing of hands.

DISCUSSION

This patient presents with a very common problem: an elderly man with a significant medical disability who has lost his main means of support. Primary care physicians must frequently deal with elderly patients with such problems. The patient has already attempted suicide once and since the patient readily admits that nothing has changed, he may very well attempt suicide again. The videotape leaves many things unsaid. We have no knowledge what he was like before his first suicide attempt. Was he under the close care of a physician? Could his first suicide attempt have been predicted and prevented? We do not have a complete physical exam. However, it appears he is confined to a wheelchair and has significant arthritis.

I have been asked to discuss this case from the perspective of the practicing physician. Physicians usually start by eliciting a complete history, doing a physical exam, and ordering appropriate tests before beginning therapy. Because of the potential risk of suicide in this patient, our approach must be altered.

A. Recognize Suicide Risk. As a primary care physician in approaching this case, I believe the most important aspect is to quickly recognize that this patient is still a suicide risk. Patients who have previously attempted suicide are more likely to attempt suicide again than those who have never attempted suicide. In fact, 60 percent of all people who have committed suicide have made a previous suicide attempt. This alone should make us highly sensitive to the possibility that this patient may attempt suicide again. The patient, however, has several other risk factors as well.

He is elderly; he is male; he shows obvious signs of depression, his wife who had been his main support recently died; and the patient is now living alone without a strong support system. The patient also has significant medical problems. All of these factors make this patient a high risk for a repeated suicide attempt.

In such cases, it is important for the physician to question the patient to determine if he has thoughts of suicide. The physician should be frank but understanding. The topic may be introduced by inquiring about the patient's feeling of hopelessness and can proceed along these lines: "Well, I see that you are feeling very low. Have you considered hurting yourself as a way out of your troubles?" "Do you sometimes feel that you would be better off dead?"

If the patient acknowledges thoughts of suicide, the physician must learn whether the patient has plans for putting them into action. "Do you have a specific method in mind when you have these thoughts?" "Have you thought about when and where you might do it?" "Do you have a gun or are you thinking about pills or some other way of hurting yourself?"

Generally, the more concrete the patient's suicidal thoughts — with a method or specific strategy selected — the greater the chances that an attempt will be made.

The idea that the physician may plant suicidal ideas in a patient's mind by asking questions is unwarranted. The danger of failing to identify a real suicidal intent by skipping questions about suicide is a much more serious problem.

B. Protect the Patient. If the physician has a high suspicion of suicide, he must act promptly and appropriately to protect the patient. This patient should be hospitalized immediately if he is not already in the hospital. It is important that a potentially suicidal patient not be left alone but be under constant observation. If the patient is not considered a high risk for suicide, he may be left in the care of his family or friends as long as he is under constant observation. Since our patient lives alone, he should be hospitalized. Any patient who has attempted suicide or who is a high risk for suicide should be referred to a psychiatrist promptly for treatment.

C. Contact the Family. If the physician has a suspicion that the patient may be suicidal, the family of the patient should be interviewed separately from the patient. The family can often provide additional information that can aid in the diagnosis and treatment.

D. Make Diagnoses. Once the patient has been protected, the physician will then be able to obtain an in-depth history and a complete physical exam. At this time the physician can look for other risk factors and precipitating problems. All medical problems and medications the patient is presently taking should be carefully documented.

E. Treatment. Since our patient shows evidence of significant depression and has attempted suicide, he should be under the care of a psychiatrist. He will probably require antidepressant medication. The primary care physician should work closely with the psychiatrist. Any medical problems should be treated.

F. Discharge Planning. When the patient is ready for discharge, careful consideration should be given to his living arrangements. This patient should not be allowed to move back to his trailer by himself. Other possibilities should carefully be explored with his family and friends. If suitable accommodations cannot be found with family or friends, serious consideration must be given to nursing home placement or other types of residential care programs.

G. Follow up. Finally, it is important that patients such as this have careful follow up. He should be seen on a regular basis following discharge from the hospital to make certain things are going well, that his depression is being treated and that he has no further suicidal ideations. Follow up is an important responsibility of the primary care physician.

In summary, the primary care physician must have a high index of suspicion of suicide in any patient that has a large number of risk factors. Once the physician has a high degree of suspicion, he must act quickly to protect the patient. Once the patient is in a protective setting, a more careful history and physical can be accomplished, looking for other risk factors and precipitating problems. The physician should work together with other members of the health care team to help the patient resolve these medical and social problems. Good discharge planning is essential to make sure the patient is in a protected setting. Finally, adequate follow up is important to make sure that the support systems are working well and the patient has no further suicidal ideations.

Suicide is a serious concern in our society today. There are at least 25,000 deaths per year in the United States by suicide. Because of the social stigma attached to death by suicide, this is probably an under-reported figure. Of the many risk factors listed above for suicide, one of the most important is depression. About three-quarters of all people who actually kill themselves are depressed at the time they do so. Feelings of helplessness, hopelessness, worthlessness, or guilt about some real or imagined fault often lead to thoughts of suicide. About ten percent of people with major depression end their lives by suicide. For this reason, it is important that all health care professionals constantly be aware of the risk factors. It is also important that health care professionals be aware of the role of depression in suicidal patients and have a high index of suspicion for patients who might be depressed. Physicians who are busy and forced to do rapid histories and physicals can frequently miss the diagnosis of depression in a patient. Major depression (utter hopelessness, an abiding misery, feelings of worthlessness and guilt, profound psychomotor retardation, suicidal thoughts) is often easy to diagnose. However, minor depression and reactive depression may be far more subtle and more difficult to diagnose unless the physician is willing to spend more time with the patient, be a good listener, and have a high index of suspicion.

If the physician is suspicious of depression in a patient, an in-depth history and physical is warranted. One of the first considerations must be: Is the patient suicidal? If the physician considers the patient possibly suicidal, everything must be done to protect the patient as discussed above. If the physician feels suicide is not a risk, then the workup can continue:

A. *Present History.* Patients with depression frequently present with a wide array of non-specific complaints. Loss of pleasure in things once enjoyed, loss of energy or loss of initiative are most common. Other complaints include inability to sleep or sleeping too much, changes in eating or bowel habits, dimunition or loss of sex drive and feelings of sadness or anxiety. Patients with depression frequently come to the physician because of a wide array of inexplicable somatic complaints. Headache, backache, abdominal pain, constipation without apparent cause often accompany depression. Repeated office visits or vague aches and pains in which no apparent cause can be found should raise the suspicion of depression.

B. *Past History.* The physician should inquire carefully about previous history of depression, recent medical illness, or any medication the patient may presently be taking. Special consideration should be given to antihypertensive medications such as reserpine, methyldopa, clonidine, and propanodol, and to oral contraceptives.

C. *Social History.* A careful social history should investigate family or marital problems, dramatic changes in life circumstances, financial problems, alcoholism, or recent loss of a loved one.

D. *Family History.* The family history should inquire into whether there is a history of depression or suicide among any blood relatives.

E. *Physical Exam.* A careful physical exam will look for supporting evidence of depression such as psychomotor retardation or agitation, as well as a sad appearance. The physical exam will also look for organic disorders which may present with depression. This includes: 1) endocrine disorders such as hypothyroidism, adrenal insufficiency, and hyper-parathyroidism; 2) metabolic or nutritional disorders such as anemias due to iron, folate, or B_{12} deficiency, electrolyte disturbances, and malignancies of the pancreas or intestine; and 3) neurological disorders such as multiple sclerosis, normal pressure hydrocephalus, and tumors of the temporal lobe.

Once the physician has diagnosed that depression exists and the patient is not suicidal, he must determine the best means of treatment. In general, if the patient shows evidence of severe depression or suicidal ideation, he should be referred to a psychiatrist. Mild to moderate depression is often treated with anti-depressants. This can be done by a psychiatrist or if the primary physician feels comfortable, he may prescribe them himself.

If however, depression is associated only with an adjustable disorder, such as the recent loss of a loved one or a temporary setback in his personal life, usually all the patient will require is a kind, careful, and compassionate listener. The primary care physician, if he so wishes, can provide this. Usually allowing the patient to ventilate, spending some time with the patient, and showing interest will usually carry the patient over. If the primary physician feels he does not have the time nor the interest to provide this type of therapy, the patient should be referred to a psychologist or psychiatrist. Even with adjustment disorders, anti-depressant medication may be required on a short-term basis.

If depression is thought to be secondary to medication, the medication should be adjusted or changed. If the depression is thought to be due to some secondary organic disorder, that organic disorder should be treated by the physician. Even if the depression is thought to be caused by the medication or an organic disorder, anti-depressant medication may still be indicated.

In summary, depression is a common problem that is often unrecognized by non-psychiatric physicians. Patients rarely admit they are depressed, and the signs and symptoms may be subtle. Yet, with a high degree of suspicion and careful listening, a physician can usually make the diagnosis. Severe depression or depression with suicidal thoughts should be referred to a psychiatrist. Mild depression or depression associated with adjustment disorders may be treated by the primary care physician or referred to a psychologist or psychiatrist.

Depression: Psychological Perspective

NICHOLAS D. KOKONIS

THE SIGHT OF THIS 80-YEAR-OLD, DEPRESSED MAN IN A WHEELchair is a sight of utter despair. I see in this old man a case of agitated depression — a state of helplessness, hopelessness, worthlessness, and self-accusation. Feeling unloved, possibly rejected, this man is experiencing what psychologists have called "existential vacuum."

When faced with such a patient, one asks: "Is there a purpose in depressed behavior, a struggle to accomplish something that will improve his situation and reduce the force of his distress? When I work with a depressed individual, I like to reconstruct his whole life pattern so as to have a better understanding of the forces that have impacted upon him. I like to interpret the man's depression spell as a reaction to loss: the loss of a loved person, a congenial group, a supportive system. The loss might be of a more subtle, symbolic nature. Regardless of who the person, group, or institution was, the significance of the loss is in the fact that it reanimates terrible childhood experiences that have to do with loss of the mother's affection. And so, in this old man's depression, there is a meaning: In this man's hell of mental illness, I see a cry for love and a cry for meaning. I see a display of helplessness and a direct appeal for the affection and security that have been lost, in losing his wife. The agitated depression syndrome, which I believe clearly describes the behavior and emotional dynamics of this man, perhaps needs a little bit further explanation. It is a state of mind in which thoughts of death are prominent and suicide is a real danger.

Patients who suffer from agitated depression cannot keep still, cannot sleep, can only pace up and down, often moaning and sighing, ringing their hands or pulling their hair. The very existence of this syndrome, this variant form of clinical depression, makes it clear to us clinicians that dejected moods and underactivity do not necessarily go together. Agitated depression seems to combine depressed mood and anxious tension.

However, this picture of depression is complicated by the angry hostility which is directed against the deserting person, in this case, this man's wife, and by guilty fear that this hostility has actually caused the desertion. In the psychological evolution of symptoms, repentence soon gains the upper hand, so to speak, and the rage turns against the self. The patient becomes very self-critical, his unending self-criticism being intended as an act of expiation. He will fully accept the blame for the anger, then confess his unworthiness and attempt to deserve again and win back the lost affection.

However, in many patients these emotional tactics are likely to miscarry. The self-punishment becomes very painful and the despair unbearable, even driving the patient to suicide, before the attempted expiation brings any sense of restored love.

The depression spell can be conceived as the man's attempt, however misdirected, to repair the situation that has been created by the serious loss of supporting love. And so, in the present disease we have a situation which is like a drama whose first acts have been played before the lights have gone up on the stage.

Studies of depressed patients indicate that a vulnerable point exists in the organization of their personalities: They are very dependent upon their principal "love objects." They show an acute dependence on a high income of supportive love and affection and cannot tolerate frustration or disappointment from this source. They require, it seems, a constant supply of love and moral support from a highly valued love object. This creates a weakness in their personality makeup, which affects their sense of competence. As children, they show a special need for the approval of others. When young, they seem to develop a technique by means of which they obtain approval rather than developing a sense of self-worth or self-esteem that might have sustained them in the years ahead, especially the young adult and adult years.

This man's crisis is a psychological, social, and spiritual crisis at the same time. He probably experiences a certain emptiness frustration, that life has no meaning at this point. Faced with the unavoidable (suffering, dying) this man is probably experiencing what Eric Erickson calls "despair." As he looks back upon his life as a series of missed opportunities and misdirections, now, in the twilight years, he probably realizes that it is too late to start again. For him, the inevitable result is a sense of despair at what might have been.

have been. His personality lacked the necessary strength to face his predicament. In this regard, he is not like Socrates, Ghandi, or even Martin Luther King — when he said, almost on the eve of his assassination, — "I don't mind . . . my eyes have seen the promised land." Instead, this man cries for love and support; he cannot do it alone.

In working with an individual like this man, one is especially reminded of the fact that health and happiness, as well as disease and disability, derive not only from man's bodily constitution and the physical environment in which he lives, but also from his psychological and behavioral interactions with the people, who in his family, neighborhood, and state, comprise his social world. In order to thrive, human beings must draw upon certain "psychological supplies" such as attention, affection, approval, and control. Without an appropriate balance of these supplies, man may suffer from forms of "psychosocial malnutrition" which can produce results as disastrous to his health as physical malnutrition induced by dietary imbalances.

However, there is a very significant difference between material resources and psychosocial supplies. The fact that most material resources can be held in the hand, weighed, and analyzed by physical means has made it relatively easy to recognize, characterize, and measure them with scientific precision. Psychosocial supplies, on the other hand, pose more of a problem because they comprise various forms of interpersonally transmitted information concerning such matters as being valued, being the object of attention, being controlled, and being reasonably secure about continuing to receive these supplies in the future. It is the recipient who decides whether he is being valued, attended to, controlled, etc. The fact that this decision is not always made evident to an outside observer by the behavior of the recipient may at time pose difficulties for the clinician/diagnostician.

Now, some facts: Depression is the most common psychiatric disorder treated in office practice and in outpatient clinics. Some authorities have estimated that at least 12% of the adult population will have an episode of depression of sufficient clinical severity to warrant treatment. Prompt diagnosis and treatment of this condition is obviously a measure of health concern. Complete recovery from an episode of depression occurs in 70 to 95% of the cases. About 25% of the younger patients recover completely. After the initial attack of depression, 47 to 79% of the patients will have a recurrence at some time in their life. After the first such type of depression, most patients have a symptom-free interval of more than three years before the next attack. Approximately 5% of hospitalized manic-depressive patients subsequently commit suicide. The notion that the patient who threatens suicide will not carry out the threat is fallacious.

How shall we treat depression? Medical therapy for depression is at least as ancient as Homer, who related in the Odyssey that Penelope took a drug to dull her grief for her long-absent husband. But as a psychologist, I am particularly interested in psychotherapy, or psychological treatment of depression. For this point of view, I would recommend the follwing steps. First, the precipitating or aggravating environmental factors that may be blocking the patient's effort to rest or to relax should be removed.

Second, the patient should be helped to become aware that inordinate conscienctiousness stems from inner feelings of guilt, from an over-strict conscience, and from keen feelings of insecurity. He should be encouraged to expect less of himself, then to develop a more nonchalant outlook on life.

Third, in addition to reeducation, reassurance, and explanation, the clinician should also explain that the illness is self-limiting and that the person will get well. Advice should be given to the family and friends. It should be explained that the illness requires rest and relaxation, and that the patient must avoid anything that increases his tension and anxiety. Occupational therapy and bibliotherapy are also likely to prove very helpful. The patient should be encouraged to read to relax and to improve his mind and personality. I very often recommend that my patients read the Bible, as I have personally found that to be a very comforting experience. I maintain a list of bibliotherapeutic references, and I share this with my patients when appropriate. My psychotherapy program is individualized according to the patient, the phase of his illness, and the intensity of the symptoms. I am almost certain that depressed individuals need to be understood, need to develop their hope, and need to be supported. Therefore, supportive psychotherapy, as contrasted to insight oriented or exploratory psychotherapy, is likely to be more helpful with very depressed individuals. Reassurance, ventilation and catharsis, guidance, and environmental changes are among the techniques I rely upon. In a case like this individual, I would also consider hospitalization as an extreme form of environmental change.

In my frequent contacts with an individual who is as depressed as this man, I would be guided by the precept that suffering ceases to be suffering in some way at the moment it finds a meaning.

Physical remedies and treatments are of immense value. Psychotherapy has opened up a new field through which many distressed have found healing, but both together cannot of themselves integrate personality, for neither can relate it to reality. One of the healthiest performances of a man's life is the performance in which, even though it be through utter despair or through the persistence of a restlessness which can find no other satisfaction, he turns himself toward God and begins to quest for the one who all his life has been seeking him. Indeed, man's restlessness is a sign of that search. One of the basic tenets of one form of psychotherapy, called "logotherapy," is that man's main concern is not to gain pleasure or to avoid pain, but to see a meaning in his life. That is why a man is ever ready to suffer under condition that he is sure his suffering has a meaning. In this regard, I know no wiser and no truer words in the world than the words of Saint Augustine: "Unquiet is our heart until it rests in Thee."

I consider myself exceptionally fortunate to have been invited to this founding conference. I am very thrilled about the mission of our new Association. It seems to me, as I work with the emotionally disturbed, that modern psychiatry has forgotten the person. Every man, especially the man for whom I have been focusing my remarks, needs a relationship with someone — a meaningful relationship, and we all need a meaningful relationship with each other, as professionals. It is a real blessing for all of us to have the insight and strength to develop the Orthodox Christian Association of Medicine, Psychology, and Religion.

Depression: Religious Perspective

NICHOLAS KROMMYDAS

OUR LORD CAME INTO THIS WORLD TO "BEAR THE INFIRMIties" of us all. If he indeed was Christ, then one of his outward signs would be to heal the sick. In Matthew 4.24 we read, "So his fame spread throughout all Syria and they brought him all the sick, those afflicted with various diseases and pains, demoniacs, epileptics and paralytics and he healed them."

Christ's healings were a demonstration both of his divinity and of his mercy and love for man. That the power which he brought into the world should not be lost with his ascension into heaven, he commands his disciples and followers, "Heal the sick, cleanse the lepers, raise the dead, cast out devils; freely you have received, freely give" (Mt 10.8). This power has been and remains in the Church through the Holy Spirit and continues through disciples, priests and all those who are called to administer the true healing that God can only bring (Mk 6.13).

Throughout the centuries those who have understood Christ's command and his charge of healing have been given the special gift of restoration of health in his name. They are the spiritual fathers and directors who have followed their Master totally and therefore have received the grace to carry out this awesome command. The spiritual father, in our Christian tradition, is the equivalent of the modern doctor-counselor. He is not just a knowledgable individual, but one who lives in the very presence of Christ, having experienced the healing power of God. He is the one who by example, compassion, and love seeks to bring those who suffer to the one true Physician.

I would therefore like to elaborate first on what the traditional Orthodox understanding of spiritual direction is and then sketch for you some of the basic characteristics that a spiritual father should possess. Finally, I would like to offer some brief comments on the film we viewed today in light of what has been said.

Saint Basil says that for every ailment, there is a cure. Our God is a healing God, as Scripture clearly and repeatedly shows. A spiritual director — "Abba" — or spiritual father — "gerontas" — is one who has a first-hand experience of healing in his life, as a result of his relationship with Christ — the true healer. This is the person who is girded with the gift of transmitting God's healing power within the faith.

The tradition of the Fathers, especially the Desert Fathers, was that if one is not touched by brokenness, it is difficult to heal brokenness. Thus, the spiritual director is constantly, actively, and vigilantly listening to the promptings of the Holy Spirit as he hears or rather lives the pain of the one who suffers.

When we come in touch with the Holy Spirit, we realize its main purpose, and that is to divinize; to lift the *whole* person as one — body, mind, and soul — and help him to become whole, or integrated. The Church, therefore, encourages this process of spiritual direction because in this very special relationship of spiritual father-spiritual child or director-directee, not only does the individual work out his need, but he also becomes sensitive to God's grace and the spiritual challenge of life.

The Fathers of our Church emphasized that man needs God and his grace. When one grows distant from him, when one drifts, then sin and all its attributes rush in. We thus need healing and *metanoia* — a return, a change of heart, whereby we realize that at our innermost self, we *crave* God. In our Orthodox faith, we can say we crave not just an abstract God, but one who loves and has compassion for us, so that he gives himself and of himself. We always, therefore, conclude and yearn for the *Parousia* — the Kingdom — the presence — the synergy of being together with God, whereby we are united in one with him.

A spiritual director is not a professional in the sense of the word, but rather one who is grounded in humility, charity, openness, and love. He ought to be rooted in the Spirit of God and the divine. His aim is to bring others to God and thus introduce them to salvation which can only come from God. He ought to love deeply and take on others' sufferings as his own, and he can only do this because he is anchored in God and thus, can bring healing to that which ails and is broken. In his relationship with others, he does not try to solve problems, but rather tries to create a relationship of love and attentiveness to God's Spirit in order that it becomes the soil — the arena, where true healing takes place. The word "compassion" means entering into one's suffering and above all, this word expresses the spiritual father's domain.

Although he incorporates various skills and techniques learned from other disciplines, the true gift of the spiritual father is *diakrisis* — discernment and concern as to the workings of God's Spirit and thus revealing the true state of our spiritual being. Using Scripture, the Tradition of the Fathers, the Church, and knowledge from other areas to lead one to *wholeness* and to "the knowledge of truth," we can therefore say that direction is form-free.

All this takes place within a certain context — the Church. The Church is the true place where we become true listeners of God's voice. The Church is the people of God witnessing to the active presence of God in history. It is there where we are reminded of what is really happening. In its yearly cycle of events, it unfolds to us the Christ event and keeps us rooted in God by making his active presence known to us. It is here where the healing power of the Spirit can be mystically received, especially in the form of the sacraments and by the fact that we belong to Christ's Body — his Church — his community.

Comments on Depression

I have tried to set the stage whereby we are able to differentiate between the various disciplines in response to a cry for healing. By no means is the religious isolated or insulted from other disciplines. As a matter of fact, in the case presented to us today, I would strongly recommend both medical and/or psychological assistance for this man.

It is important to provide for those in need and to have such individuals who share and understand God's healing process. Most times, referrals become decisive and suggest that only one method of healing is available or possible and therefore block true and total healing of the whole person.

We must point out the following:

First: That the person came to the priest and his church and therefore has certain expectations and trusts that healing can come from there (Christ — the Church).

Second: That the person has taken a step towards facing a problem, discussing openly his depression and therefore is open to receiving direction — forgiveness, sacraments, and support of a Christian community, i.e. Church.

Third: Because he has chosen to come to the Church, he is familiar with various ways that healing is administered — through Holy Communion, confession, unction, prayer, etc., and this can be of assistance to him.

Fourth: The link that will make all this happen and bring him true healing, by introducing him to the true healer of body-soul, is the *spiritual father*, whose knowledge and skills in various disciplines will support his recovery and whose love, concern, and compassion will see to it that he is directed not to a particular person or method of healing only, but to a true and total saving of his soul. Spiritual guidance in this case and in all cases is not just crisis intervention, but a continuous process, the movement to God and in God.

PART THREE
GENETIC ENGINEERING:
WHERE DO WE DRAW THE LINE?

Introduction

PAUL TALAGAN

A NUMBER OF YEARS AGO, WHILE TRAVELING SOUTH FROM my hometown in Wyoming, I would often pass a certain cattle ranch that had a large sign above its feedlot. The sign read, "Genetic Engineering." I thought about that term "Genetic Engineering," and I knew what genetics was from my biology courses and I knew what engineering was, but somehow, as I thought of those two terms together, I became rather puzzled. It was not until much later that I began to understand the significance of what I read on that sign.

The possibility for increasing food production for a hungry world that genetic engineering offers us, as well as offering the potential for curing inheritable disease, is both a blessing and an exciting possibility for humankind. That sense of being puzzled, however, returns to me as I consider in the light of my faith, the potential outcome of genetic research and engineering as researchers expand the limits of science further and further.

Is it appropriate and fitting that humankind employ knowledge and technology to manipulate human life — that which is so sacred to us? For the Orthodox Christian, the question remains, "Where do we draw the limits?"

Genetic Engineering: Scientific Perspective

PETER H. DIAMANDIS

MAN'S REACH HAS EXTENDED TO THE OUTER LIMITS OF THE universe: he has probed into the inner confines of the atomic nucleus and has altered the molecular basis of life itself. Time and time again barriers which were once thought sacred have toppled, and regions of knowledge thought known only to God have become incorporated into man's amassed knowledge. Today, as molecular biologists contemplate improving on life, astronomers theorize on the origins of the universe, and scientists plan for the transplantation of human life on to other worlds, people are beginning to raise serious questions about our activities. What right does man have to move in these directions? Were we meant to have the key to the most basic essence of God's creations? Does our exploration into the mystery of the universe comply with God's plan? Should we spend such exorbitant funds and time on this type of research when thousands die each day from hunger and exposure?

Without doubt the field of research which most challenges our ethical and religious values is genetic engineering. Today, molecular biologists have unraveled a significant portion of the DNA genetic code — that instruction set which directs growth, metabolism, and reproduction in every cell in the body. Work in genetics has progressed to the point where scientists can actually consider improving upon what already exists . . . what God has created. Though pretentious, it may soon be within our abilities to produce larger farm animals which provide more meat, larger eggs, or more milk. It is also conceivable that families with a trait for genetic disease may have their genes corrected. Thus, thalassemics or sickle cell carriers could bear children without fear of passing on the disease. In the near future, technology may lead to greatly extended lifetimes tending toward immortality. The term "designer jeans (genes)" may take on a new meaning as parents preselect what their children should look like — what gender, how tall, what color, how smart. Is it heresy to think that we have the right to consider such moves? Where would it stop? Surely being able to correct genetic disease is both moral and ethical, but once we can control a few genetic outcomes, wouldn't parents want their children to be taller, more muscular, more intelligent, with blonde hair or with green eyes?

In this presentation I hope first to give you historical background to demonstrate how rapidly our understanding of genetics has been developing. I hope to also present a simplified overview of what genetic engineering encompasses, what exists as the current state of the art, the near-term plans for treating diseases in humans and, finally, a glimpse at what this revolutionary technology might provide for us in the next few decades. Primarily, I would like to point out many of the dilemmas which genetic engineering might create for us in the near and not too distant future.

Historical Perspective

The science of genetics, the understanding that a living creature's appearance is controlled by inherited instructions called genes, was established in 1865 by a modest Austrian monk named Gregor Mendel. Unfortunately, as with most significant breakthroughs, Mendel's ideas were not initially accepted. It was not until the early to mid-twentieth century that our rudimentary understanding of genetics began to progress. Limited by our inability to peer into the microscopic world of the cell's nucleus, scientists were forced to understand genetics through crude animal breeding experiments in which mutations and characteristics such as height and color were followed from generation to generation. It was not until 1953 that the scientists finally understood what, in fact, the gene was composed of, for in this year, Drs. Watson and Crick discovered the structure of DNA (Deoxyribonucleic Acid), the very stuff of life.

Even though we knew about DNA and about genes over thirty years ago, genetic engineering, the ability to move genes around — cut them out of "this" peace of DNA and stick into "that" — did not develop until this last decade. It is only recently that we have developed the tools and the understanding to find one gene amongst the fifty thousand that we all have. Likewise, our ability to isolate the gene, cut it out, read it like the words in a book, change it to fit our needs, and insert it back to the cells of our choice is less than ten years old. Thus, we can see that genetic engineering is perhaps the most recent, as well as one of the most powerful, of modern day technologies.

Basic Theory of Genetic Engineering

The human body is made up of cells, billions and billions of them. Each of these cells takes on special functions — some of them carry oxygen, some fight infection, some contract, and some conduct electrical signals. Regardless of their specialized function, they all stem from a very basic design and, in fact, they all stem from that one cell formed during your conception — the fertilized egg. The shape you have today, the information which determined the structure of each cell in your body is packed into the nucleus of each cell in your body.

To give you a basic understanding of genetic engineering, let me first briefly review the basic components of the cell:

Cell: The basic unit of life. Able to reproduce (in most cases) and perform such functions as respiration (energy production), growth, and internal repair. Cells of similar function are collectively known as "tissues" (e.g. bone tissue, brain tissue, epidermal, etc.).

Nucleus: Present within every human cell. The nucleus is a membrane bounded area which contains the genetic material. Also contains the machinery needed for replicating and reading the DNA.

Chromosomes: The condensed version of the genetic material. Composed of one long stretch of DNA which folds upon itself many times over. Humans possess two sets of 23 chromosomes of which one set is the sex chromosome. Some genetic diseases can be detected on this level (example: Down's Syndrome).

DNA: Deoxyribonucleic Acid. The molecule which encodes the genetic information. DNA is a continuous chain made up of four subunits. It is analogous to a language with four letters. The four letters are arranged to form words and sentences which the cell can interpret as instructions.

Genes: The basic instruction unit. Analogous to sentences in our four-letter language scenario. The cell contains over fifty thousand genes. Each gene is an instruction for a particular function. Particular genes control when other genes should be read; some genes are instructions for the cell to build a protein; and others sense conditions in the environment and decide that it's time to divide or remain dormant.

Nucleotides: The basic letter in the DNA language. There are four different nucleotides symbolically represented by the letters T, A, C, and G. The order of nucleotides is crucial for the genes to be properly understood. A change in this order (for example, TACGTG --» TACATG) due to radiation or chemical mutagens could potentially lead to serious problems.

Proteins: Coded for by genes. The basic worker of the cell. Some proteins serve as structural supports like beams in a house; some proteins contract as in a muscle; some proteins recognize other molecules in the cell and thus function as "eyes"; and some molecules function to cut and splice other molecules (the scissors and glue).

Enzymes: The name given to those proteins which recognize a particular molecule and split it at a particular point, or conversely recognize two separate molecules and bring them together in a very specific manner (the scissors and glue mentioned above).

Mutations: Changes in the nucleotide sequence which result in abnormal genes and in the final consequence abnormal proteins and cell functioning.

Inheritable Genetic Disease: A mutation which is passed on from parent to child. In the case of Sickle Cell Anemia, the mutation is an inappropriate nucleotide in the gene which codes for the protein hemoglobin.

Conventional medicine treats genetic disease by treating the symptom, and rarely the cause (i.e. the aberrant protein). The reason for this is simply that, for the most part, such direct treatment is beyond the physician's means. Thus, diabetes is managed by supplying insulin, not by replacing the genes responsible for the inadequate productions. Imagine, however, if it were possible to enter into each cell of the body that produced the abnormal protein, locate the mutated gene, cut it out, and in its place paste in the correct version. The result would be a total cure, not some temporary or palliative treatment but a permanent conversion to normalcy. Beyond this, if it were then possible to correct the genes in the germ line cells which give rise to the sperm and ova, then future generations would also be free of disease. The removal of all genetic disease is one of the dreams put forth by genetic engineering.

Today's Cutting Edge Technology

The genetic engineering and biotechnologies of today are progressing rapidly, turning the fiction of the last decades into a reality. Without going into detail, a few of the most dramatic developments bare mentioning.

Genetic engineered drugs have recently entered into the marketplace. Produced by bacteria or yeast, pharmaceutical companies are developing new, advanced antiobiotics, cheaper, purer forms of insulin, and cleaner immunizations against hepatitis.

As physicians and geneticists have started to understand the genetic basis for disease, it has increasingly become possible to perform simple tests to *predict* whether or not an *individual is inflicted or a carrier* of a particular disease. The tests performed are painless, the researcher needs the DNA from only a few cells. Off hand, such tests seem helpful — after all, this information could be of critical importance to genetic counselors in advising a couple with a family history of a particular disease. However, when closely examined, some ethical questions arise. What if the individual being tested is only a few months old such as in amniocentesis and a genetic abnormality is discovered? Abortion? What if the disease is one of later life? There are, for example, genetic diseases which can strike down or kill a person in later life (e.g. Huntington's Chorea). A genetic test showing a positive result in that individual's life might destroy any hope of leading a normal existence until the time when the disease becomes apparent.

Today, the ability of certain technicians to perform microminipulation of subcellular structures is truly phenomenal. Over the years it has become possible not only to isolate an ovulated egg, but also to inject genetic materials into its nucleus. What this all comes down to is two very impressive capabilities: *invitrofertilization* and *cloning*.

Invitrofertilization, as most people know, is a reality. It has successfully been performed numerous times. It is, however, still in its primitive state of development. In the future, it will no doubt be the case that genetic information used for the fertilization is very carefully selected by the explicit directions of the parents rather than the random union of sperm and egg.

Cloning is the ability to take one cell from an individual and from it reconstruct the entire person. This technology has existed for years with certain lab animals such as frogs, mice and horses, and unsubstantiated rumors tell of two successful cases with humans. Nevertheless, even if the rumors are false, the technology to accomplish cloning in humans is not far off. Science fiction has recounted for years how clones could be raised for the sole purpose of organ transplants. When your heart, liver, or kidney is beginning to fail, your clone will be ready to provide you with a perfectly compatible replacement. Is it moral? After all, the cell that started the whole clone off was yours! Does the clone have a soul?

The total genomic content of humans is huge. Human beings have over 50,000 genes directing their development, metabolism, and reproduction. In terms of "nucleotides," the basic building blocks which make up the letters of the genetic code, the human has trillions. Of these trillion letters which describe man in detail, we have only deciphered about one percent. Over the last two to three years, our ability to "sequence genomic DNA" — in other words, read these letters, has increased immensely. Recently, it was suggested that an intensive effort to completely read and record the entire genetic code of humans be undertaken. Such a project would require hundreds of man years and billions of dollars, and would produce essentially an encyclopedia filled with a four-letter alphabet describing man in the most basic detail.

What are the religious implications of such an event? Man would be reduced to an extensive description, a series of letters, a complicated instruction booklet. Molecular technology not only allows us to read a DNA sequence, but also to create one. Biologists have successfully strung together nucleotides to create stretches of DNA. Is it then possible that a geneticist given enough time with the proper equipment and the encyclopedia of the human genetic code could, from commonly available chemicals, create a human being. Obviously the issue is much more complex than slapping together the proper molecules, but this begins to raise fundamental questions about the essential nature of man. What more is the human being than a very complicated assemblage of the proper atoms? What and where is the spirit or the soul? As we begin better to understand the human body at the most basic levels, such questions begin to weigh very heavily.

Perhaps one of the most graphic presentations of genetic engineering was the insertion of an additional growth hormone gene into a line of lab mice. This new breed of "super mice" was approximately twice the size of the original breed. Such experiments represent only the beginning of our abilities to enhance or diminish certain characteristics of living organisms. Such manipulations may provide livestock which are larger, healthier, and tastier.

The final and perhaps most important consideration of today's cutting edge technology is the area which has been termed "gene therapy." In simple terms, gene therapy is the process of providing a patient with a normal copy of the gene he or she does not possess. In practice, a patient with a particular genetic disease (for example, sickle cell anemia) would receive an injection of highly modified viruses which would seek out specific cells in the body and infect them. In the case of our example, the virus would seek out the bone marrow stem cells which are the precursors to the hemoglobin producing cell. After infecting those cells, the viruses would insert their DNA into the nucleus, as many viruses normally do. The beauty of this system lies in the fact that the viruses were initially modified to remove the pathogenic genes of the virus and replace them instead with the gene of choice (in this case, the normal hemoglobin gene). Thus, the virus has in essence functioned as a messenger to identify the proper cells and deliver to them the particular gene of interest. Today, this technique, though promising, still has a number of unsolved problems such as regulation of the genes once inserted into the genome.

Looking into the Future

As fantastic as genetic engineering seems, as disturbing as some of the results appear, it is only the rudimentary manifestation of a much more complex and powerful technology known as molecular engineering or nanotechnology. Molecular engineering is a field whose implications we are just now beginning to understand. The technology is one which manipulates objects on the level of the molecule and atom — thus, the prefix "nano" (nanotechnology). One can hardly imagine what is possible if we obtain the capability to control the assembly of structures on such a fine level.

For the moment, I wish only to stretch your mind, your understanding of reality. Scientists in the field of molecular engineering arc today working on molecular computers. Computing machines, perhaps as powerful as your personal computers (PC's) which arc microscopic — so small that they fit within one hundredth (1/100) of the volume of the average human cell. In addition to these "nanocomputers," theorists are contemplating the construction of nanomachines — molecular-size machinery with the ability to recognize certain atoms or molecules, pick them up, move them about, and attach them to other building blocks. Such nanomachines are not inconceivable. In his book *Engines of Creation*, K. Eric Drexler, a research affiliate of the M.I.T. Space Systems Laboratory, points out that ribosomes, enzymes, bacterial flagella, ion pumps, and a variety of natural subcellular structures represent nanomachines. Drexler demonstrates how this technology can be used to assemble molecules atom by atom, in any combination of interest, thus producing nearly every conceivable substance or device within the limits of nature. Such a technology will surely revolutionize healing.

Medicine has been, and is today, a very gross and inexacting technology. We deal with some diseased organs by cutting them out; we deal with cancers by baking them with radiation; and we treat diseases with chemicals which have broad and many times unknown interactions. We do this because it is the best that we can do. Healing, in its ultimate form, is not just palliative, but instead the act of returning the body — each and every cell — to its perfect state of being. Imagine for a moment if we were in fact able to do this — remove the accumulated waste and repair the protein cross linking damage caused by aging in every cell of the body — the result is summarized in one word: immortality. When asked about the prospect of molecular technology, Dr. Gene Brown, Professor of Biochemistry at M.I.T. said, "Given sufficient time and effort to develop artificial molecular machines and to conduct detailed studies of the molecular biology of the cell, very broad abilities should emerge. Among these could be the ability to separate the proteins in cross-linked structures, and to identify, repair, and replace them."

Genetic engineering and molecular engineering will give humanity unbelievable capabilities. But, as with any technology since the advent of fire, the ability to accomplish the greatest good goes hand in hand with the ability to do the greatest harm.

In the future, this technology *will*, without doubt, give us life-saving drugs, cure some genetic diseases, and give us a better scientific understanding of the human being. In the future, this technology *may* lead to immortality, new life forms, and on the negative side, germ warfare, and abominations of the human form. In the future, we must learn where to draw the line. Genetic and molecular engineering may in fact not have any limitations other than those imposed by the laws of nature. In the near term, what is needed most is educated individuals — people who do not blindly demand a stop to this research, but people who provide informed guidance, feedback, and support to the researchers and overseeing institutions which exist today. It is in this role that I hope religious institutions will become involved.

Genetic Engineering: Religious Perspective

JOHN BRECK

THE VERY EXPRESSION "GENETIC ENGINEERING" HAS AN ominous ring to it. It suggests manipulation and consequently, violation of human life at its most basic level. At worst, it conjures up images of newly created life forms, whereby a select few will achieve the status of Nietzschean "supermen" while others are reduced to humanoids that constitute an inferior servant class.

In any discussion of the ethics of genetic engineering (GE), it is important to separate fact from myth and possibility from fantasy. GE holds out extraordinary hope for improving the quality of human life by: 1) increasing the quality and abundance of crops and livestock; 2) by producing insulin, interferon, hormones, vaccines, etc., for use by humans; and 3) by making available products to improve the environment, such as enzymes to break down industrial wastes, fertilizers developed from nitrogen rather than from oil, and inexpensive, relatively pollution-free automotive fuels.

Yet, like many products of modern technology, GE is inherently dangerous. If it promises to correct genetic anomalies, improve intelligence, and provide offspring to infertile couples, it could serve as well — presumably in the near future — to produce genetic hybrids, a master race, or the ultimate weapon for use in germ warfare. The question "Where do we draw the limits?" is therefore an urgent one that the Church must raise *now*, and to which she must give a clear and firm answer. And such an answer must somehow guarantee both legal enforcement and continual ethical review. In this brief paper, I can only state the nature of the problem and attempt to indicate how much limits should be determined.

We should begin with a few basic definitions. The science of *genetics*, which came into its own at the beginning of this century with the rediscovery of Gregor Mendel's laws of heredity, is the branch of biology that studies the "genes" or units of the chromosome which transmit specific traits and genetic defects. Between 50,000 and 100,000 genes are located on each of the 46 chromosomes contained within the nucleus of every human cell. Often referred to as the "blueprints" of our heredity, genes are composed of segments of deoxyribonucleic acid (DNA), which in turn comprise four chemical subunits that determine the "genetic code" of inherited characteristics.

The science of *eugenics* investigates, develops, and applies methods for improving the genetic code of particular individuals and the human "gene pool" as a whole. A distinction is usually made between "negative" and "positive" eugenics. Negative eugenics refers to various forms of intervention that seek to eliminate genetic defects. It begins with "genetic screening" to discover defective genes within the parent that might be transmitted to the child; or, by the process of amniocentesis, it seeks to discover whether the fetus is afflicted with abnormalities such as Down's Syndrome, the XYY Syndrome, hemophilia, spina bifida, or cystic fibrosis. "Genetic counseling" based upon that screening then recommends an appropriate course of action: contraception, abortion of the fetus, or where possible, "genetic surgery" to correct the problem *in utero*. Negative eugenics, then, aims essentially at prevention and therapy.

Positive eugenics, on the other hand, strives to improve what are understood to be normal and desirable traits, with the purpose of creating a superior human being. A fundamental moral problem arises here with the determination of "criteria of excellence": who decides, and on what grounds, which traits are in fact the most desirable? In our production-consumption oriented society, where economic forces prevail and competition is exalted as a supreme virtue, traits such as intelligence, ingenuity, and aggressiveness would surely be valued above the human qualities Jesus identified in the Beatitudes (Mt 5) or Saint Paul included in his list of the "fruit of the Spirit" (Gal 5). Positive eugenics raises other ethical problems as well, in that its methods and goals would encourage widespread use of in-vitro fertilization (IVF), embryo transplants (ET) into surrogate mothers (SM), and artificial insemination using the sperm of an anonymous donor (AID) rather than that of the husband (AIH).

Because both negative and positive eugenics can in principle employ some of the same methods to achieve their aims (e.g. IVF, recombinant DNA techniques, or "gene splicing"), it would seem more appropriate to label them respectively "therapeutic" and "innovational" eugenics. For, ironically, an Orthodox moral perspective would judge "negative" eugenics as potentially capable of attaining positive and desirable therapeutic results, whereas so-called "positive" eugenics would have to be rejected as unwarranted tampering with human life created in the image and likeness of God. While Christian people can and ought to support research into the area of therapeutic eugenics, they cannot morally condone other forms of research in which the basic principle of self-determination is violated by techniques of manipulation.

Does GE, then, constitute therapeutic or innovational eugenics? The concept of "eugenics," like the concept of euthanasia, tends to promise more than it can deliver. Insofar as acceptance of euthanasia can lead to "death on demand" through the willful taking of human life by suicide or authorized murder, it violates the very principle of a "good death." In fact, given the tragic nature of death as both a cause and a consequence of human sin, it is questionable whether the expression "good death" has any meaning at all, or whether it is merely a contradiction in terms. However that may be, the Church's prayer is for "a Christian ending to our life." Yet, we also pray that that ending be "painless, blameless, and peaceful." Appropriate therapy — using certain drugs, even when they might impair reason and hasten death in terminal patients; and allowing various forms of medical intervention, including withdrawal of life-support systems — is therefore acceptable, and is in fact required by an Orthodox approach to bioethics, to permit the natural dying process to occur with a maximum of consciousness and a minimum of suffering. If properly defined and practiced so as to preserve and enhance the spiritual, mental, and physical well-being of the terminally ill patient, what is called "passive euthanasia" can be morally acceptable in certain cases.

Therapeutic eugenics is to the beginning of human life what appropriate passive euthanasia is to its physical end. Similarly, innovational eugenics corresponds to active euthanasia and must likewise be condemned. Ethicists are particularly concerned with the risk of narrowing the human gene pool and the consequences of circumventing the natural evolutionary process by employing innovative techniques in the conception and development of human life. Still more serious are the implications of innovational eugenics for spiritual growth: the interior movement towards union with divine life that we term *theosis* or divinization. Such growth is only possible within the fallen created order through a process of continual repentance and the free exercise of moral choice that permits the practice of such virtues as altruism, kindness, generosity, devotion — in a word, Christian love. A growing number of specialists in the fields of eugenics and sociobiology, however, hold that such moral virtues are in fact biologically determined, that like vices such as greed and egotism, they are the direct expression of our individual genetic programs.

For years, debates have focused on the relationship between genetic factors and environment in determining human behavior ("Is intelligence related to race?"; "Are criminality and violence due to an extra Y chromosome?"; etc.). Orthodox anthropology rejects *a priori* any "hard determinism" that would reduce a human being to a caricature of himself by denying the person the God-given freedom to make choices, to establish personal relationships, and to exercise the spiritual options of repentance and reconciliation.

What should our criteria be, then, for determining the limits within which GE may be ethically practiced? And how can we, as Orthodox Christians, gain the leverage in our society, marked as it is by a certain "techno-idolatry" and passion for the new and untried, to ensure that the Orthodox position will be heard and, where necessary, legally enforced?

Because of the gravity and urgency of the problem posed by potential misuse of GE technology, the first step should be to create an inter-Orthodox ethical review committee. Such a committee, selected from among physicians, scientists, and theologians who are familiar with bioethical issues, should be given the official approval and blessing of SCOBA. Furthermore, it should receive adequate funding from our various jurisdictional treasuries to provide research facilities and secretarial staff needed to monitor and to disseminate information to the Church and to the general public. Close cooperation with similar groups within the Roman Catholic and Protestant churches would be indispensable. A multitude of questions arises with such a suggestion: how to determine the criteria for selecting members, to ensure both competence and the absence of vested interests; how to guarantee adequate financing; how to develop appropriate methods for acquiring and publicizing relevant information, and so on. Good will and informed concern, however, can resolve such problems and remove inevitable obstacles.

The work of such a committee should be complemented by other initiatives: creating special seminary courses in bioethics, open to a broad spectrum of the public; including position papers in church publications and popular journals; and generally raising the level of consciousness of our Orthodox people to the potential for good as well as to the dangers inherent in genetic research. It would be as morally wrong for us to hinder research and the application of proper therapeutic methods which result from it, as it would be to remain silent in the face of evident abuses.

This means, however, that we as Orthodox must work not only to inform our faithful of new developments — both promises and risks — in the field of GE. We must also seek appropriate ways and means to press for *adequate legislation* and other safeguards, both for ourselves and for the public at large.

Finally, we must be willing to engage in an effort of continual review. Technology is developing today at a prodigious rate, especially in the areas of genetics and microbiology. Certain techniques already exist which Orthodox Christians simply cannot accept and still remain faithful to the Gospel and Tradition. Such techniques include abortion (with the rarest of exceptions where the life of the mother is truly endangered), forced sterilization to prevent the transmission of undesirable genetic traits, artificial insemination using the sperm of an anonymous donor (AID), IVF involving the freezing and storing of embryos, surrogate mothering, and in general any technique by which man attempts to recreate man in his own image. Each of these proves inadmissable because each inevitably dehumanizes the persons involved. Although IVF-AIH may in some cases be ethically acceptable, should the Church not rather urge its members to *adopt*, given the masses of eligible children throughout the world? Whereas cloning — the artificial production of an identical twin — holds out tremendous promise for agriculture, must not the Church condemn it as grotesque genetic manipulation when it is practiced on human beings? While the embryo has no discernible level of consciousness, and might appear to be an appropriate subject for abortion or genetic experimentation, does not the Church celebrate liturgically the *conception* of her Lord and the saints, thus placing ultimate personal value on the conceptus not only as a viable human person, but as a bearer of the divine image?

While these and similar questions must be given firm and unambiguous answers by Christian people and by the Church as a whole, they should not be allowed to blind us to the truly marvelous possibilities that the science of GE offers us today for the betterment of human life tomorrow. Because it is in its infancy, and yet new developments occur so rapidly, continual reassessment of bio-possibilities and bio-hazards is imperative. As with any ethical issue, each particular case must be judged and evaluated on its own terms, within its own context. This does not mean, however, that we are bound by a "situational ethic." Orthodox moral theology is based upon absolute truths — upon Him who is the Truth itself and its judgments can and must be informed and guided by Holy Tradition as well as by the potential inherent in any particular technological achievement.

Orthodox Tradition demands absolute respect for the integrity and freedom of the person. Determining the appropriate limits to GE, or to say any other technique or process that can irreversibly affect human nature itself, can only be done appropriately and faithfully insofar as such respect for the person guides our judgments from the moment of life's conception until its fulfillment at death.

PART FOUR
MIRACLES: SCIENTIFIC AND RELIGIOUS
REFLECTIONS

Introduction

GREGORY PHELAN

IN OUR STUDY OF THE MANY INTEGRATED FACETS OF HEALing at this symposium, one subject stands out as one of the most important, or, at least, the most dramatic: miracles. When someone considers healing from a Christian standpoint, the first thing that comes to mind is miracles. Christian healing and miracles are almost synonymous. Beginning with our Lord's many healing miracles as related in the Holy Gospels, we all know of thousands of cases of miraculous healing throughout the long history of the life of the Church. These miracles testify to the promise of Christ that we who are His followers will heal the sick, raise the dead, and cast out demons (Mt 10.8). They testify that the Kingdom of God is at hand, breaking through into this dark world. All of us have experienced a miracle at one time or another. Permit me to relate to you a healing miracle which I recently experienced in my own pastoral ministry.

Not long ago, I received a young man into the Orthodox Church whom we shall call "John." John had been married for several years to a woman who was herself a lifelong member of my parish. His zeal for the faith was astounding and very refreshing. He pursued his catechetical studies with enthusiasm, calling me frequently on the telephone with this or that question. He was always present at the Divine Liturgy with his wife and children, in spite of a long drive from a distant suburb.

On the day of his chrismation and reception of Holy Communion, a small party was planned after the Divine Liturgy to celebrate his joining the Church. In the ensuing hubbub, he forgot to read the post-communion prayers of thanksgiving which he had been taught to do. He remembered this on Wednesday of that same week, so he sought out his prayer book, sat down on his sofa, and quietly read the prayers. When he finished, he walked out into his backyard and, he told me later, was so astounded by what happened that he almost fainted.

About ten years ago, a severe viral infection of his nasal and respiratory tract destroyed his sense of smell. Since that time, he had been able to smell nothing. His sense of taste was also greatly diminished. There followed a difficult period of psychological adjustment to this handicap. When John walked into his backyard, which he had landscaped with shrubs and flowers of many varieties, he told me that he was almost overcome by the sweet fragrance flooding his sense from the flowers. Indeed, he went from flower to flower, burying his face in each one, incredulous at what was occurring. Of course, he also said that he could now smell all odors, good and bad — including his wife's cooking! Thus, a miracle.

A miracle, a joyous epiphany here and now of the kingdom of God, a shining forth of the truly real among the darkness of the less real. Miracles are a true taste of God's promises to us.

Miracles: Scientific Reflections

THEOHARIS C. THEOHARIDES

THE WORD MIRACLE, ΘΑΥΜΑ IN GREEK, OBVIOUSLY DENOTES something that generates wonder, as it was used by Homer and Hesiod in various settings. The English word derives from Latin to denote the same thing, but primarily an event that occurs in the human experience by a natural agency for which we really have no explanation. We therefore turn to divine or supernatural intervention. Greek tragedies many times ended by what was called divine intervention, or ἀπὸ μηχανῆς θεοῦ. Over the years, there have been numerous attempts to explain the miraculous in medical or realistic terms[1], an attempt which culminated in the *Psychiatric Study of Jesus*.[2]

The world around us clearly is one of the best examples of a miracle, and our attempt to understand it comprises a series of small miracles in their own right. Our ability to try to explain the world around us clearly derives from our analytical powers which depend on the neurons, the specialized cells, that make up our brain. These neurons have the theoretical ability to make as many connections in a lifetime as there are molecules in the universe, a power which is really stupifying and constitutes, at least in my mind, a miracle in itself.

The fight between the powers of evil and good are notions that have been carried through the centuries and have colored the study and possible understanding of miracles. The curing of the possessed

---

[1] E. Le Bec, *Medical Proof of the Miraculous: A Clinical Study* (London, 1922).

[2] A. Schweitzer, *The Psychiatric Study of Jesus* (Boston, 1948).

by Christ is one of the best ways of depicting how a miracle may occur. This miracle, as depicted on a sixteenth century icon from Mount Athos, shows something concrete in the sense that our Lord can expel a demon from an epileptic patient with a gesture and with words. On the extreme opposite of this simple gesture is the scientific unpredictability of the universe. When young Einstein developed the theory of relativity, he proclaimed that the beauty of the world around us clearly cannot be explained by our very poor ability to predict where some atoms might jump from one place to another.[3] It is this inability to understand a very complex and miraculous universe which makes us so skeptical about a simple gesture from our Lord being able to cure a complicated clinical entity such as epilepsy.

The detail of the icon stresses the gesture of our Lord in trying to make contact both verbally and physically with the patient. This may be considered one of the first attempts to somehow indicate that there is *human contact* or *communication* in such phenomena which would otherwise be called miraculous. In another sixteenth century icon from Mount Athos, one observes the dialogue between Ioannis the Theologian and Cynops, leader of the demons. During this presentation, a number of possessed people are actually cured through a *dialogue*; the miraculous cure is therefore endowed with some human qualities such as the power of speech, so characteristic of present-day psychotherapy.

In a scientific paper that was entitled "Ticket to Heaven," the authors examined some communities in Ethiopia.[4] These communities drew on people considered outcasts of society. These individuals exhibited characteristics such as the lack of ability to conform to society's norms. Such characteristics would today be considered to reflect severe psychiatric disease, and these individuals would probably need to be institutionalized. Instead, they were operating fairly efficiently within the context of that mini-society. One may call this phenomenon a miracle of love, which brings us to what I consider the ultimate miracle: the fact that God embraced us all with such love that he assumed human nature and was sacrificed for us. This love of his, then, crowned by his Resurrection, is the most miraculous event known. Love, and love for God, could then be a very powerful source in our trying to explain miracles. How

---

[3] "Conservative Einstein," *New York Times* May 4, 1935.

[4] R. Giel, "Ticket to Heaven. Psychiatric Illness in a Religious Community in Ethiopia." *Soc. Sci. & Med.* 8 (1974) 549-56.

could such love possibly allow us to have a vision of the miraculous? A recent television advertisement may help explain this. It shows a glass filled with water to the midpoint, and the commentator says: some consider this glass half-empty and some consider it half-full; however, one could see it as the way to permit a rosebud placed in the water to blossom.

How a miraculous process works may be depicted by taking up the example of dermatography which has been used over the centuries as proof of the miraculous. This is a phenomenon where the skin of certain individuals has the ability to show letters when you press it. There is a population of cells in the skin called mast cells, which are full of granules.[5] If these cells are stimulated, they undergo an explosive release of their contents; it was not until the early 1950s that release of at least one molecule, histamine, from such cells could clearly explain the swelling of the skin which resulted in a welt-like appearance of letters on the site where such letters had been pressed on it.

The Greeks first thought that the life force residing in the site of the diaphragm (φρήν). Interestingly, in biblical Greek this term is retained in the word ἄφρων, which denotes something foolish; it was later used in the term *phrenology*, the "science" of studying behavior by examining the shape of the skull. Today, we try to understand the brain by focusing on certain specific areas and how distinct molecules bind to it. Such molecules can influence the brain in very different ways as to create or alleviate pain or changes in mood.

Since our brain communicates with most organs of the body, central effects of what we might collectively call the brain will alter drastically the physiology of the rest of the body. Central effects in the brain could therefore possibly explain such disparate findings as they might occur in what we would otherwise call miraculous cures. Some examples may help illustrate this point. Take migraine headaches, for instance. This is possibly the most excruciating type of headache, which even today is still associated with another condition: epilepsy. It is presently believed that some major veins going to the brain first constrict and then they dilate. It is during the first phase of constriction that retinal vessels constrict and lead to a pattern of visual hallucinations, in other words, flashing lights and honeycomb shapes, which has given rise to the belief that such in-

---

[5] T. C. Theoharides, "Mast Cells and Precursor Protein Molecules," *Persp. Biol. Med.* 26 (1983) 672-75.

dividuals may indeed be possessed. It is during the second dilation phase that patients feel the throbbing pain, and mast cell mediators are thought to play a major role in the pathophysiology of these events.[6] We can, therefore, see how characteristics that can clearly be explained in biological terms have led to what otherwise would have been called possession and how the cure for such individuals might have been called miraculous.

Migraine patients are presently treated by substances called ergot alkaloids.[7] It is interesting to note that these substances derive from a fungus growing on wet rye, and ingestion of it could lead to a condition termed convulsive ergotism which is characterized by hallucinations. It was these substances that gave rise to the massive hysteria of young women in the sixteenth century in Salem, Massachusetts.[8] Unfortunately, both the psychologists of the time, the physicians, and the priests collectively considered these young women witches [9] and condemned them to the torch. It is a miracle to me how we can be so blinded in our assumptions of our understanding of human nature.

In the case of epilepsy, it is known that a small area in the brain could become epileptogenic. Such areas generate electrical activity which can cause the symptoms of epileptic seizures. We now know that our brain cells show what is called plasticity: they have the ability to change their characteristics almost entirely and therefore have innate ability to change so that one may in principle be able to either alter or bypass the epileptic site altogether. We still have no idea how such an event happens, but the fact that we do not understand it does not mean that there might not be a cure for something mental that today might still be called miraculous. The same holds true for mental illness.[10]

Our age has been defined as the age of anxiety.[11] We have

---

[6] T. C. Theoharides, "Mast Cells and Migraines," *Persp. Biol. Med.* 26 (1983) 672-75.

[7] L. Lasagna, "Pain and Its Management," *Hosp. Practice* 21 (1986) 92C-92X.

[8] M. K. Matossian, "Ergot and the Salem Witchcraft Affair," *Am. Sci.* 70 (1982) 355-57.

[9] P. J. Swales, "A Fascination with Witches," *The Sciences* 22 (1982) 21-25.

[10] J. Miller, "The Myth of Mental Illness," *The Sciences* 23 (1983) 22-30.

[11] M. Clark et al., "Drugs for the Mind," *Newsweek*, November 12, 1979, pp. 98-104.

powerful drugs to tamper with such conditions; however, the most common of these classes of drugs, the benzodiazepines, at high doses cause depression. Indeed, practically all major classes of drugs have depression as a major side effect. In a sense, some of the major conditions that afflict the human race medically seem to derive from what we do to ourselves and to the environment; recognizing and trying to correct such factors then, as removing a medication that might have caused depression, may at times be taken to constitute miraculous cures.

Our efforts to understand nature should also demonstrate humility about what we know and what we can master. In a seventeenth century icon from Crete, Saint Anthony is depicted holding a scroll which reads: "He who is humble can humble the demons." Humility is a lesson appropriate to the modern medical scientist as well. For instance, aspirin has been called the wonder drug of the twentieth century. Yet, it was used by Hippocrates around 300 B.C. when he asked pregnant women to chew on bitter willow leaves to ease the pains of childbirth. It was not until 1887 that the German firm Bayer synthesized acetyl salicylic acid by extracting salisylic acid (the active ingredient in aspirin) from bitter willow leaves.[12] The recognition, therefore, of what took more than 3,000 years or so to understand should indicate that it may take another 3,000 years before we understand processes we still call miracles.

---

[12]M. Clark and M. Hager, "An Old Drug's New Miracle," *Newsweek* May 10, 1982, pp. 91-92.

Miracles: Religious Reflections

JOHN MEYENDORFF

I BELIEVE THAT AT THIS LATE HOUR, IT IS SOMEWHAT DIFficult for all of us to speak of deep spiritual matters and miracles, but I am given courage by the fact that the Lord performed his first miracle at the wedding feast where the people were drinking wine and having a good time. It is important to believe that God is with us in whatever we are doing. I will shorten what I wanted to say and point at two or three major presuppositions about what we, being Christians, call miracles.

The first major presupposition which I think is essential for us to realize is that the world in which we live, the life which is ours, our experience of the spiritual and physical reality around us, something which we know very well, is not exactly what God intended for his world to be. This is one of the basic presuppositions of the entire Christian faith: the world was created at the beginning, but there was some kind of derailment almost immediately which was contrary to God's will. Something in creation, somewhere, in which we are involved, very directly, existentially, and deeply, is wrong. The will of God is being betrayed. If one takes the world as it is around us as normal, as the one that God created, one realizes that one has to allow for God creating evil, creating suffering, creating death, creating all that agony, and all this terrible tragedy which surrounds us every day. But we know that God does not create evil. God is not responsible for evil. Evil, therefore, is a kind of external element in the reality of the cosmos, which God does not want to be.

I will not go into further explanations of the reasons for that situation. All philosophers, all theologians have tried to explain the origins of evil, but no one has succeeded. Nevertheless, it remains as one of the most real facts of our life. Many people actually lose their faith because of that reason: "If God wants the world to be the way it is, I don't want that God." Many people reason that way and, of course, have a point. Now if you take the tradition and the thought of the Fathers, you discover specific pointers explaining the condition of the world as it is to what is wrong about it. Both the New Testament and the tradition of the Church speak of death as being the major, the last enemy. The Book of Revelation of Saint John tells that the "last enemy" will be destroyed — death. Death is what it is: the last, ultimate enemy.

In Scripture and in Christian thought, death is our physical death indeed, but it is also something greater than that. There is also a spiritual death and a spiritual mortality which is even more real than physical death. There is a spiritual death and spiritual mortality which is even more real than just the physical death. But both, somehow, are connected.

Death is something which God did not want — but which is nevertheless a central reality in the life of the world and in our experience. Furthermore, we can say at this point that death has a moral dimension. It is related to sinfulness. This connection can be described in a variety of ways. This is not a place for a complicated theological lecture, but only an occasion to point at something central in the Greek patristic tradition. Death is seen by the Fathers of the Church as a central factor of our existence, which makes sin inevitable. The Fathers are much more sophisticated than one thinks: they do not simply believe that death is a punishment for sin, that we all die because we are bad people, as if God were "pushing the button" or "pulling out the switch" so that we may die — No! Death is a cosmic reality which is almost personalized, an objective reality in the world which also creates sinfulness. How? It makes it inevitable because it transforms the entire reality of the world into a desperate struggle for survival.

Darwin had a point when he described the world precisely in such a way. Are not we all struggling for survival all the time? The author of the Epistle to the Hebrews, in chapter 3, speaks of the fear of death as something which is the origin of sin. Sometimes I use this example with students: If you have two people who were in a shipwreck, and they are in a raft, they have one pitcher of water and one piece of bread, and they have three weeks to go until they reach the shore. If they divide the water and the bread, there's no chance of survival; they will both die. But if one of them eats the bread and drinks the pitcher of water, he has a chance. So what happens?

They have a fight. The stronger survives and gets to the shore. This parable explains well the relations between nations, or individuals. It can also explain the fact of our constant search for security. We all, for example, need to have a bank account. I have a monthly check because I have a job. Now that gives me relative comfort, but what anxiety, what anguish if it does not come: my security, my life, and that of my family depend on it! But is it "ultimate security?" There are millions of people who are hungry. The fact that I just had a good meal, and I have some security for tomorrow and for my family only delays the day when I will experience the universal power of death.

So, the temporary, illusory security given to me by my monthly check, by my insurance policy, and my savings does in no way solve the ultimate problem of life and death, but it inevitably creates injustice and therefore sin. I survive temporarily, but at the expense of others. This is why St. John Chrysostom once wrote that property creates injustice.

Now this does not square well with capitalistic ethics, but it is the rule by which our world exists. There is some injustice in the very fact that I have that illusory security. But why do I pretend that I have the right to have this meal? Because otherwise I am going to die. My health will deteriorate, so in addition, I have a pension plan and am very much concerned about the security of the future and all that struggle for existence. But it is always, always at the expense of others. There is injustice in my struggle against death. I know that it is a very temporary struggle, and that ultimately it just prolongs my life, but it does not solve the real problem. Now, we are coming to our topic: Which event does solve the problem in terms of what we believe?

The only event in fact which does solve it is the Resurrection of Christ. That is why this is the "good news." The Apostles went out into the world and proclaimed the good news that death is no more; death has been conquered by death. There *is* a hope. The two people on the raft could have securely shared this bread and water. They may have both drowned, but if they believed in God and Christ, they would have eternal life. It is because they fought against each other — not because they lacked food — that their death became the ultimate death. The only true miracle which really matters is Christ overcoming death. It is really a miracle, in the sense that it is an intervention of God within this fallen world and a sign of his power which can be shared. It is really, authentically the only true miracle. All the other events which we call miracles are only signs and pointers to that one miracle.

Take even all the miracles performed by Christ in the gospels. These were all temporary events. Lazarus rose from the dead, but he died again. The people who were healed from some disease, like the epileptics, fell sick again. One of the most fascinating things in the New Testament is that you cannot be a Christian and believe in God and not believe in miracles, but all the miracles beside the Resurrection of Jesus Christ have only a relative significance. During the Middle Ages, people attributed miraculous qualities to all sorts of healings of this temporary nature, but now scientists and doctors discovered that they can be performed with drugs or surgery. They were miracles, but so are the feats performed by medical science. In each case, both are feats of only temporary relief.

It is obvious that in the history of humanity, many more people were actually healed by drugs and doctors than by miracle workers. There are miracle workers who perform some miracles from time to time to strengthen our faith, but millions and millions of other miracles are performed by people who just try to help their fellow being and, so, science has a justification. It is actually a secondary matter whether these healings are performed by science or by extraordinary means, by special divine interventions or by scientific means. All these miracles are aiming at one goal: to improve the quality of human life, to show concern for human suffering, and to try to alleviate it. This solidarity between people is something which in itself can be seen as a sign of the victory of the Kingdom of God which is to come. But the ultimate, final miracle is only that which was performed by Christ. Saint Paul says that if Christ is not risen from the dead, our faith is in vain. Christ's Resurrection was a real intervention of God in the reality of life which gives content to our faith. Now the last point which I would like to make is the following. If we really believe that the world as it is now is not the world in the state which God wanted it to be, that it is a corrupt, fallen world, then miracles and healings are partial restorations of what God wants it to be.

God certainly wants this world to be good. He created heaven and earth, and said that "it was good." But then, afterwards, the world collapsed, not by His fault, but through an intrusion of other factors. All the miracles performed by Christ were actual but partial restorations of the original order of creation. The world is created according to the will of God, and God acts to fulfill that plan, not to modify it all the time. This is the theological argument and background for what we discussed this afternoon in connection with genetic engineering. To restore God's plan is fine — but to improve on what God did is questionable. The problem is to know the difference between God's will and man's ambition and presumption.

You people who practice medicine are in fact doing the same thing which our Lord Jesus Christ did — except, of course, that you are not God, and you see that your means are limited. But your goal is the same. It is in his name, in cooperation with him, by participation in his love for fellow creatures that you do what you do. Actually, the difference between what is a miracle or a successful medical operation is perhaps a little abstract. Perhaps we should not even be too concerned about it. People are looking for miracles. They are sometimes superstitious, and we have to be tolerant about that. But the Lord Jesus Christ was not very tolerant of those people who looked for miracles for miracles' sake. "Miracles," he said, "will not be given to them except the miracles of Jonah the prophet," i.e., the miracle of the Resurrection that is the only miracle which is given free and is the ultimate miracle.

In practice, what is important in our concern for human healing is to discover that this is a concern of God also. God created the world, and he is the one who wants to restore it in goodness. He performed the ultimate miracle and sacrifice by becoming a man, by rising from the dead, by conquering death. But we live in a period of human history where human freedom is still given to us to do the right thing. We are called to cooperate with him, to try to heal, and to share in his concern for the healing of man, both of his soul and in his body with our limited means which continually increase with the progress of science. This is also part of the will of God because finally, man is an image of God. Man is given the possibility to participate and to share in the healing and creative power of God but only within the limits of God's will. If we want to be better than God, if we want to improve on what he did, the real danger comes in. Moreover, this is where the really demonic power appears. It is Satan who wants to be like God and, in fact, be better. He cultivates such aspirations among us also. He tells us to eat from that tree and not from this one, so that we might create a "superman" on our own. This is really the demonic temptation. It is my duty, as a theologian, to point to it, define it, and to talk about it. But you who are engaged in the responsible talk of scientific research and practice, you have the more difficult task of taking the right options. Let us work together to acquire the same vision, the same intuition. This common work is our ultimate responsibility before God and humanity today.

PART FIVE
AIDS: ACQUIRED IMMUNE DEFICIENCY SYNDROME

Introduction

ANTHONY VASILAS

FEW SUBJECTS HAVE CAPTURED THE PUBLIC'S ATTENTION IN recent years as have the infectious diseases. The news media constantly keeps us informed about Legonaire's Disease, herpes, Toxic Shock Syndrome and most commonly, AIDS.

Not long ago, the medical profession and the public thought that infectious diseases were under control — tuberculosis, small pox, polio, the pneumonias, and many others. Each time resistance to antibiotics appeared, new antibiotics developed. However, now AIDS has come to the fore and as yet, no treatment has appeared.

Despite dozens of public announcements about the nature of AIDS and how it is or is not transmitted, myths and fears about this fast-growing public menace continue to increase. AIDS is creeping into the population of the non-drug using heterosexuals. In some areas of New York City, the most common infectious disease in newborns is AIDS.

Our panel promises both to update us concerning the medical, psychological, and religious dimensions of this problem and to place the interdisciplinary perspectives into an Orthodox Christian framework.

Human Immunodeficiency Virus (HIV) Infections and Acquired Immunodeficiency Syndrome (AIDS): Impacts on Lifstyles in the 21st Century

GEORGE J. PAZIN

THE CLOSER ONE GETS TO THE HIV-AIDS PROBLEM, THE greater one's concern grows, not only because of AID's but also because of the impact it will have in the future. As the epidemic spreads, more people are being brought closer to the problem, and its ramifications loom larger for everyone.

Although medicine, and virology in particular, has made remarkable progress in the past few decades, it is not apparent whether a vaccine, a cure or even a highly effective therapy for HIV infections and AIDS will be forthcoming in the near future. Clearly, as the twenty-first century approaches, HIV infections and AIDS have already had a great impact upon many lives and lifestyles and it seems likely that they will continue to do so in an even more dramatic fashion.

My expertise lies in the area of microbiological infectious diseases, which gives me a medical perspective on the problem but any thoughtful physician must realize that the current AIDS problem has psychological and spiritual dimensions as well. Therefore, I will share with you my insights from all three perspectives.

THE MEDICAL PERSPECTIVE

Virological Aspects

When dealing with a disease caused by a virus, it is critically important not to overlook the virus itself. In the case of AIDS, the virus that causes the disease is human immunodeficiency virus, or HIV. It is surprising, but apparently true, that HIV is a relatively new virus. The earliest evidence of the virus comes from a few positive blood samples drawn in central Africa in 1959. In the United States, there is evidence that a few persons were infected with HIV in 1978. (A single case was reported to have tested positive for the

HIV as early as 1969 and has received nationwide media publicity, but the case has not been reported officially in the medical literature.

Let's digress for a few moments in order to answer a few questions regarding viruses.

What is a virus? Simply stated, a virus is a sub-microscopic "package of chemicals" that has genetic material in the center and is surrounded by a protective coat with or without a lipid — or fatty — envelope on the outside. The HIV happens to have this outer envelope. It helps one to understand viral infections if one realizes that viruses are not alive.

If viruses are not alive, how do they function? The virus does nothing outside a cell. However, if it attaches itself to an appropriate cell, it fuses with that cell. Once inside, the genetic material of the virus redirects the cell to make viruses instead of the usual things a cell needs to remain alive. The viral takeover of the cell is injurious and often results in cell death. If enough cells die, the whole body is damaged. In the case of HIV, the virus infects and destroys the key cell in the immune system which ordinarily protects the body from infections and tumors.

So why does it matter that HIV infections and AIDS are caused by a virus? Viruses are transmissible from person to person. However, because they are not alive, viruses tend to be passively transferred. Viruses such as HIV, which have lipid envelopes, become inactivated rather easily outside the body, especially if they become dried out.

The main cell infected by HIV is a cell in the blood, so it appears that the HIV must gain access to the blood to infect a person. Thus, HIV is not highly contagious but, on the other hand, it may spread during a single exposure if it is properly innoculated. Because viruses execute their damage within cells, it is quite difficult to inhibit viral reproduction selectively without damaging other cells in the body. Surprising progress has been made with respect to therapy directed against HIV, but it is clear that treatment involving zidovudine (Retrovir, formerly called azidothymidine or AZT) is only partially effective. HIV is a difficult virus to make into an effective vaccine, and it is not clear whether an effective vaccine can be at all.

The Medical Aspect

As noted above, HIV attaches to and fuses with the key cell in the immune system — the system that acts as the body's protection against infections and cancers. As a result, many persons who are infected with HIV become highly susceptible to severe, life-threatening infections or unusual forms of cancer. Not everyone who is infected with HIV develops AIDS, but of those who develop AIDS, not one has had his/her immune system return to normal, with the possible exception of one patient with AIDS who received a bone marrow transplant from an identical twin. Although we may treat some of the infections or cancers for a time, most persons with AIDS succumb within two or three years.

All persons who are infected with HIV are potentially *able to infect* persons with whom they share blood, body fluids, or tissues, regardless of whether they have developed AIDS or remain asymptomatic.

Infectious Disease Aspect

AIDS would be a fearsome disease if it were of unknown etiology, but the fact that it is caused by an infectious agent that is transmissible from person to person adds an important element that on the one hand complicates disease control but on the other hand, presents important opportunities for control. The transmissibility of the causative virus contributes to the public's concerns and, to some extent, to its hostility.

Although the spread of HIV creates a major social health concern, an understanding of what is involved in the spread of infectious agents enables people to avoid the infection. In general, the spread of infectious agents such as HIV involves 1) exposure to the virus; 2) its inoculation into the body; and 3) one's susceptibility to the virus. Operationally, until a vaccine is developed (and we should not depend upon this happening), everyone must be considered susceptible to HIV at any time.

The two elements involved with spread of infections that are modifiable are *exposure to* and *inoculation with* HIV. Exposure is necessary, but not sufficient, to establish an infection. If one avoids exposure to the virus, one does not need to worry about preventing inoculation. However, one may not be totally able to avoid exposure to the virus. Fortunately, inoculation is an important additional factor that determines whether exposure may lead to infection. With respect to HIV, inoculation is usually accomplished when the virus is forced into the body through the skin or lining surfaces during sexual intimacy or via the injection of virus into the body during the kind of needle sharing associated with intravenous drug abuse. Receiving contaminated blood, blood products or organs directly into the body are relatively uncommon, but important, additional means of becoming infected with HIV.

The behavior associated with male homosexuality and intravenous drug abuse provide both the exposure *and* oculation requirements for the spread of HIV, but these requirements can also definitely be present during *heterosexual* behavior as well.

Although casual or close personal contact with an HIV-infected person may result in exposure to the virus, if inoculation does not occur, one does not become infected. On the other hand, unprotected sexual relations with an infected person is clearly risky. Exactly where the dividing line is between casual or close personal contact and intimate sexual contact is not addressed very often. In my opinion, intimate contact is present at that point where HIV in a body fluid may be inoculated directly upon a mucosal membrane or lining surface, such as the inside of the mouth. Therefore, during passionate kissing, it might be possible for the virus to be transferred from an infected person to an uninfected person if the mucosal lining is inoculated. Whether the virus can be spread by passionate kissing remains an unanswered question, but I feel that the seriousness of AIDS or HIV infection (serious in terms of its contagiousness as well as its potential for disease) dictates that it must be assumed that the spread of HIV via passionate kissing is possible and must not be ignored in our efforts to avoid infection with HIV.

The Medical Impact of HIV Infection and AIDS on Lifestyles

One's *premium* should be to avoid exposure to and perhaps even more importantly, to avoid *inoculation* to HIV. The medical significance of this infection dictates that thoughtful people should have "RISK ELIMINATION, NOT RISK REDUCTION," as their goal. Although latex prophylactics may provide an effective barrier to the genital exchange of body fluids containing HIV, direct exchange of saliva containing HIV may provide the functional equivalent of a "small leak." It seems, therefore, medically advisable to reserve passionate kissing to serious or monogamous relationships, not promiscuous ones. Most public health-minded physicians have concluded that casual sexual relations are not advisable in many areas of our country. A conservative approach would also question the advisability of "casual passionate petting." Medically speaking, courting should become more and more thoughtful, deliberate, and geared in "slow motion" rather than to the casual "anything goes," "let's try it" attitudes that prevailed in the sexual revolution of the 60's and the 70's.

The Psychological Perspective

Two events during the 1960's had a profound effect upon the

collective psyche of American society. The development of the oral contraceptive and the landing on the moon gave Americans an attitude that "anything goes in without consequence" and "humankind can do anything it sets its mind to." Although some people looked upon these achievements with a sense of wonderment and responsibility, many did not. Much in the way that the Challenger tragedy destroyed the over-confidence found in our space program, genital herpes and AIDS have shaken and now shattered our sense of unbridled sexual liberty. A false sense of security and freedom has given way to the anxiety of "What's next?"

Self-doubt, shame, and perhaps even guilt are commonplace. Self-help support groups are meeting almost constantly throughout our nation to assist the afflicted, infected, and at risk to cope with this unprecedented threat to their psychological and social well-being. If people are willing to change their behavior in order to eliminate risks of exposure to and inoculation with HIV, a true sense of security is still possible.

The Spiritual Perspective

Throughout history, persons concerned about the spiritual dimensions of life have warned that humankind must use their mental capacities to ask, "What is correct and proper? What is right?" Interestingly, if we examine spiritual guidance in light of recent developments, the profound wisdom of morality in protecting people against known and unexpected, unknown dangers to health is manifest.

From a spiritual perspective, the proliferation of AIDS should reinforce an attitude of humility. Pride in man's accomplishments has been diminished by the suffering that ill-advised behaviors such as promiscuity, drug abuse, and adultery, have promulgated upon humankind.

To the spiritually-minded person, it is not surprising that spiritually-founded behavior has emerged as a sound, healthful lifestyle. Organized religion must not ignore its responsibility to bring forth its valid message of chastity, faithfulness, and true love. Persons responsible for the spiritual dimension of lifestyles must be constantly vigilant. The concept of a healthy lifestyle must be promoted in a non-ambiguous, non-confusing manner with clear and uncompromising images of proper behavior.

SUMMARY

Much of mankind's recent behavior has been exposed as spiritually, psychologically, and medically unhealthy. The desire for unrestricted sexuality and the initial pleasure brought on by drugs are compelling enticements of our age, but a thoughtful person has to be impressed by the remarkable power of counterforce that HIV infections and AIDS are exerting on society today and the even greater pressures that will be exerted in the future. Hopefully, the ominous specter of infections associated with the human immunodeficiency virus and acquired immunodeficiency syndrome will help us redirect behavior into medically, psychologically, and spiritually healthfull lifestyles as man enters the twenty-first century.

Psycho-social and Theological Concerns Related to the Care of Persons with AIDS

PETER POULOS

I WOULD HOPE THAT EVERY ORTHODOX CHRISTIAN, REGARDless of what ministry in which he or she is involved, whether the priesthood, medicine, nursing, or social work, would have some sense of what our Orthodox background brings, and how it influences the way we approach and see people in their situations. So, I would like to set the stage for my reflections on AIDS by sharing some of what I would emphasize in my own theology and in my own work.

One such point has been mentioned a number of times already throughout the conference — that the human person is made in the "image and likeness of God." I have said to student chaplains, "I don't care if she is a prostitute and she is brought into the emergency room on Saturday at 3:00 in the morning. If you are going to minister to her, you must be aware that she too is made in the image and likeness of God, even if she doesn't know it."

What does it mean to be made in the "image and likeness of God?" I think that as we study about God, get to know God, and relate with God, we begin to know more about what it means to be human because we are made in his image and likeness. I am not saying that God equals human, but some of that potential that we have of what it really means to be fully human is experienced and learned by getting closer to God and knowing God. One thing experienced and learned is that *God is love.* To love! That's basic to what it means to relate as human beings. Another is that *God is the Creator.* If you have ever watched children as they make things, you may have noticed the thrill that they experience. I have some of that in me. Nobody makes a cheesecake as good as my cheesecake. I'm sure they do. But when I make a cheesecake, there's the feeling that I formed it. There's an excitement about it that I don't get when I buy it from the store, even if their's may be a little bit better. Painting or working in the garden, for example, is also to experience part of that creating role. The other thing about God is *living in relationship*. This morning during the Divine Liturgy, you could hear it in the words. Take the Liturgy book and look from beginning to end; you are hearing about a God who lives in relationship. The three Persons of the Trinity — Father, Son, and Holy Spirit — each has a different role in how they relate to one another. God's relationship to His people is exemplified by the covenant he made with with them. Saint Paul tells us how we are to live in the Church or the community: " . . . bear one another's burdens and so fulfill the law of Christ." Living in that kind of a relationship is basic to who we are.

When we move away from those things, those God-like things, we live in sin; not sin against a God who is up in the sky, but we sin against the way we were created to live. I often use the statement, "We sin against ourselves," which leads to illness and suffering. The emphasis in Orthodox spiritual life is *living in relationship with the Holy Spirit*; experiencing more and more the presence of the Holy Spirit and being influenced by that experience. This is a very personal relationship which is basic to human life and basic to an Orthodox Christian life. Another theological emphasis is talking about people's value and worth. From where does a human person get his value and worth? From how much money he or she makes? Or from how physically attractive they are? Or how popular they are? Or from their social status in life? Or from what they do for a living? Or is it that we are children of God, made in the image and likeness of God? It's not from what we do or what we have, but from who we are that we have value and worth.

These things to me are basic in approaching patients in the hospital and in any area of pastoral ministry or in relating to people and caring for their human needs. Who is it I am going to see? Those things have to come with me — those beliefs — and influence what I am doing . . . and how I am listening and what I am hearing. So those beliefs are part of the theological framework or background for talking about hospital patients and specifically, for talking about AIDS patients.

Now let's go into the hospital and see the AIDS patients and their situation. That whole issue of relationships and how they are necessary and basic for life to have meaning is something that strikes me about AIDS patients: that their relationships are broken — immediately broken.

The patient's relationship to himself and to life is broken; to life in that we all know someday we are going to die. When we see these 85-year-old and 90-year-old patients die, we say someday, "I'll die" . . . but it's so far away. It's only when you get to be 83 that to die at 85 becomes a concern. We have a way of keeping it at a distance.

Yet, for the patient who is 27 or 35 and is told, "You have AIDS," that person is hearing a death sentence; that within the relatively near future, he is probably going to die. What probably? He *is* going to die! And so, death becomes part of his life. His relationship to life changes very quickly . . . to death. One fellow told me, "When they took my blood and I saw them put this red sticker on the vial, the sticker said biohazard." He continued, "That has stayed in my mind that I'm dirty, that I'm contaminated, that you'd better stay away from me. That image has stayed in front of me — biohazard." That's how this patient sees himself. So his relationship to himself is changing.

The type of illness that AIDS is is also very unusual. People with terminal illness usually follow a fairly consistent course. With AIDS, one of the difficulties is the back-and-forth quality to it. A person may be in the hospital for a while and then go home; however, he is too sick to work, but is not so sick that he has to stay home in bed; so he is confined to the home. His finances are dwindling down because he can't work, and he may have to get on Medicaid and other types of assistance, but it's hard to place himself. "Am I sick or am I not sick? They tell me that I have AIDS. Some days I believe it, and other times I feel so fine and think that they made a mistake. I don't have AIDS."

This whole feeling of uncertainty that becomes part of the patient's life until he gets much sicker and really feels it is what makes living with AIDS extremely difficult to manage. One of the losses that comes with the diagnosis of AIDS is the loss of independence. Most of us who are young have a need to be independent, and leaning on others is difficult. When we are no longer able to work and when we are not physically well, we need to have others there to lean on, and that's an adjustment. It's a difficult adjustment and yet it happens rather quickly. This is the loss of invulnerability — that I'm still so powerful. I feel fine. I'm young; and suddenly, I feel like an old man.

I remember a poem. It was about an elderly woman talking about the aging process. It had a sketch of her in the corner, a sketch so clear that you could see the wrinkles in her face. She was saying in the poem, "Don't look at my wrinkles; you don't need to stay away from me or be afraid of me; don't look at my wrinkles, look into my eyes — there's a little girl in here. She's still here. Relate to her. Let's talk." I sometimes think of this poem when I see young patients who in a very short time have lost fifty or sixty pounds, and they are wrinkling away. That sense of being powerful, of being able to hold off all destructive forces, is gone. From 35 or 27 or 28 or whatever, you are suddenly old, or feel it and look it.

Another loss is the loss of privacy. Many times in the hospital, what we are seeing is that the patient who is diagnosed with AIDS is in the situation where he has to tell his family for the first time that he is gay . . . as well as telling society. So something that he has been able to manage and keep as a private part of his life has suddenly been opened up. People diagnosed with AIDS have to struggle with "what do I tell people once I am well enough to go back to work after that initial diagnosis? Do I tell them I had pneumonia only? Whom do I tell? How much do I tell? How will they react to me? And that sense of privacy . . . "how much are people going to know about me, because they are going to see my physical symptoms? So a person's relationship to self and to community changes . . . and relationship is so much a part of health and meaningful life.

Some of the most striking things that we have seen are relationships with family — and how those things change. A man who was about thirty was diagnosed with AIDS. He lived with his parents in the neighborhood where my hospital is located. The family was supportive in that they came to visit him; they would buy things for him, and they did his laundry. Then the family had a meeting. They came and informed him that although they still loved him, he could never return to live with them at home because of the embarrassment and the shame that they felt. This was a situation in which they were learning that he was gay for the first time. They said, "We can't predict how the community will respond to your having AIDS . . . and we need to stay there. We are not abandoning you," they said, "but you can't live with us anymore." The social worker was talking about trying to find a place to help this fellow. That man's father came into the hospital for the first time to see him, stood in the doorway, looked at his son from a distance, stared at him and yelled out, "You faggot!" and ran away.

In terms of ministry, you are struggling with: "To whom do I minister, the patient or the father who is looking at his son and looking at the loss of his dreams." So it's a family issue. You could say that the father is terribly insensitive. Be he is struggling with his loss, that "I had a son who is a stranger to me now, and the son is going to die quickly, that the son suddenly has become a confusion to me."

There is another hospital situation, in which I did not minister, but which I raise for a particular point: The business about stress and its effects on the immune system. This fellow lived in the area where the hospital is. From another state, he was a professional guy, diagnosed with AIDS. He, too, had never told his family he was guy. He was in the hospital for one month, and the people working closely with him were trying to see what kind of resources were there for him. They raised the question about when he was going to talk with his family — and have them come to New York. The staff offered to call and he said no. I will call when I am ready. After a month he did call, but he could never accept that he was gay. He lived such an isolated life-style. He had no friends, no support system in terms of even gay friends. Very often family is not there, but people have developed friendships and the friends come into the hospital; they are the ones who take care of him when he gets out. This guy had no one. He lasted four months. He never left the hospital. He went from ICU back to his unit, to his room. Then he got worse again, he went back to ICU. Within four months, he died. So you wonder, what that whole struggle, his struggle with his sexual identity, was doing to his immune system and how quickly that he died.

The other real example is in relation to gay people. Sometimes the friends are the support. But you also have situations where the person with whom the victim closely involved, a love relationship, disappears. They go home and find a note on the table saying, "I'm sorry, but I can't handle it." One of the reasons they can't handle it, is because within the gay community AIDS is a time-bomb. People are living with the fear "Who is next?" So I look at you and I look at my own death.

This is true about all of us. That's one of our difficulties. His initial reaction for everyone dealing with death. When we talk about dealing with a grieving family, if they are going to be told that the patient died, make sure you get them in private. Why? Because they are going to want to run. You see it in the lobbies of hospitals, that family is told "I'm sorry the patient died," or as it is said in the hospital, "expired." And right away, the family will often start running down the corridor. We all want to run away from death. But this particular illness, for people in these high risk categories, is very scary, and so the abadonment is not just from family and others, but even from people with whom they were intimately involved.

The other community, or relationships, involve hospital staff. In the hospital where I work, we had a situation where it became very clear to us that on one unit AIDS patients were being treated very well because the nurses had dealt with their feelings about it. On another unit, the food was being left at the door. This wasn't for just one patient, but for all of them. A complaint was made to my department and we had to look into it. It turned out that it was the fear and anxiety of the nurses and of the dietary staff, to go anywhere near someone who had AIDS. This question speaks to hysteria, in reactions to AIDS patients.

The other affecting AIDS patients is that of homophobia. We're all raised with this notion that sexuality is a tiger and must be kept under very tight control or it will run wild, and we will destroy ourselves. And I have heard reactions from nurses, such as "they brought this on themselves." There is almost a sense that they deserve it. And I wonder about how much of that is related to the fear of homosexuality and our own struggles in dealing with our own sexuality. There's a sense that "they broke the rules. They did it. They did wrong and they deserve to be punished. They're being punished." I have a hard time with that. Working in a hospital, I have a very hard time when people say, that this is a punishment from God. As if there's a God up there with darts. This one gets cancer; this one has a heart attack; this one has whatever. If you follow that reasoning through, that is a very cruel image of God. I personally could not accept such a God. And yet the patient is struggling with the same issue. This business of homophobia exists within gay people too. And so, somebody who thinks he has dealt with his sexual identity, now gets the illness and says, "I'm being punished because I'm gay." "I'm being punished because I'm sexual" . . .and all those things that he thought were resolved are not resolved, and that's part of what people are struggling with.

I think it's a myth that all people, all gay people who get AIDS were promiscuous. I think that's convenient in the sense that it would be safe if we could explain it in that way — and then keep the illness under control. But I think we are fooling ourselves.

An important consideration relating to AIDS question is how AIDS relates to the physician and priest. I have already touched upon this subject with the issue of blame and judgment. One of the most prevalent important that dying patients, regardless of what they are dying from, talk about, is the fear of abadonment. This fear is basic to all of us from childhood, "That mommy is going to leave and she's not going to come back again, and I won't be safe. I'll be alone here, and I can't manage." Patients need reassurance. Whether cure happens, whether restoration to health will happen or not, and if you as the physician believe it won't, and the patient also knows that it won't, the patient still needs to feel that the doctor will still be there for him. The patient wants to know, "that even though you're anxious or uncomfortable because I am so sick, and you are limited as to what you can do for me, that you'll come back. That you won't disappear . . . and that if there's pain you will try to help make the pain as minimal as possible — just to know that you'll be there."

The same is expected of priests. A critical question attending this whole ministry to AIDS patients is, are they still members of the Body of Christ? And if they are, what is the role of ministry? I suspect some of the issues that priests have around giving Communion is not only contagion but judgement. One priest said very clearly, "How can I go see that patient in the hospital, when I know the patient is gay? Going will be approval of his life style." If as a priest, your sense is that you must go and either bless or curse, you'll never get there. It is legitimate to say . . . when a person says, "what does the Church teach about . . .? my response is, "what do you think the Church teaches about . . ." Whatever they're asking about, start where the person is at and then talk, rather than by giving a lecture. So once you tell me . . ., and if your response is such that your anger at the Church is coming out, then let it come out. I'm here as a representantive of the Church, a representative of the Body of Christ, a representative of God, and if you're angry at God okay. It's okay in intimate relationships to be angry . . . and I will take it as a representative. And that your life style may present a problem for me is okay. The question is, where do we go from here? You're suffering. I'm concerned about you. I would like to be available to you in whatever way I can. Moving away from that sense of "I must bless or curse" is important because that is what blocks you from being helpful.

We are dealing with issues that are a struggle. I think it's okay in ministry to be struggling. That doesn't mean we have to stay away. It is a similar struggle that the physician has; that I come in and see you day after day and I know what I can do for you is limited. But what I, as patient, want to know is, "okay maybe it's limited, but am I sure you are going to do it? That you'll be there." Because at that period of dying, the dying patient is still alive. I'm still living.

Like the old lady said in the poem, Don't look at the wrinkles. There are days that all you are going to hear me talk about are the feelings of wrinkles that life is so difficult. But there are other days I may feel better. There are other days when I'm a little glad. There are days when I am going to want to talk about the meaning, value and worth of my life, which is coming to an end. It is a very important ministry to help people find meaning, value and worth and to witness to that by being there; by coming back again and again. My coming back to you says you have meaning, value and worth. And it is very important that people have that sense at this time in their lives.

Ministering to people who have a terminal illness is not preparing them for some place beyond the gates. Dr. Elizabeth Kubler-Ross who did many studies on death and dying, found that the people who have found meaning in life are the best prepared to deal with that uncertainty of death. And the ones who haven't, are the most frightened of it and struggle with it to the end . . . even when acceptance, at some point, of death would be the greatest blessing. What Kuber-Ross found and what I have found in 15 years of working in a general hospital, is that this is true. The people whose lives are empty are frightened of death, because they haven't found any meaning. So for you to come in and to preach to me that there's a God over there who loves me, how do I believe that? I haven't found that God here! But if I have sensed that God here and God is the Creator of life, then I can turn to that uncertainty, maybe not willingly, but with some sense of faith, that the some God who is here is there also, and that as I have felt embraced here I can feel embraced there. I think that is a ministry not only for ordained priests. I think it can influence the way a physician relates to patients, the ways a nurse relates to patients. It is the role for all of us, not only with AIDS patients, but will all patients . . . all persons.

AIDS: Moral Crisis?

MILTON B. EFTHIMIOU

"FROM IT'S FIRST APPEARANCE, THE DISEASE INSPIRED AN almost hysterical fear. Many fled from the crowded cities to the country. But they often found all doors barred, for no one wished the disease brought into his house." This was taken from a chronicle relating to one of the most dread diseases in the Middle Ages. The panic was the result of a series of epidemics which scourged Europe in the fourteenth century. Its name: the Black Death. Millions died. Medical knowledge was hopelessly inadequate. The causes of the plague were unknown.

The Church did what it had done for centuries before and has continued to do in the centuries since. It ministered to the *victims*, asking no questions, blaming no one for being afflicted. Priests, men and women, religious and lay persons took heroic risks, aware that contracting the disease meant almost certain death.

I do not compare AIDS victims to either the victims of the Black Death or to those who had leprosy. Any such comparison would be gross and not to the point. The point is the question of fear, of panic, of confusion, and of endurance. The point is that we have been caught up in what many health authorities call an epidemic, while warning us that we may have seen only the beginning, to date. Understandably, there are some who have reacted with fears close to panic. To blame them or to indict them is nonsensical. Most of them are less fearful for themselves than for their children and others they love. And why not? We always fear the unknown. We read whatever we can get our hands on about the nature and origins of the disease — and a good bit has been written about AIDS. We listen to announcements from public health officials who try to reassure us. But many live in the nagging fear that such officials are either telling us more than they really know, or not telling us all they know. And even the most trusting find conflicting accounts in newspapers and periodicals. So there is honest and understandable fear.

In the meantime, the victims suffer; their families and their children suffer. This is why the Orthodox Church must do its part to try and help, regardless of the causes of the disease, or how it has been contracted in a given case.

The Disease

This disease, which only began to be followed by the Center of Disease Control in Atlanta (CDC) in 1979, is caused by a virus labeled either HTLV-III (Human T-Cell Lymphotrophic Virus Type Three) or LAV (Lymphadenopathy Virus). The virus itself is not the real killer. It destroys the body's immune system and thus renders the person prey to a variety of life-threatening illnesses. These illnesses are called "opportunistic infections" since they take the "opportunity" of an impaired immune system to enter the body and do their damage. The most common of these infections is a deadly form of pneumonia found in 64 percent of the cases. *Kaposi's sarcoma*, a skin cancer, occurs in 24 percent of the cases. Once diagnosed, the disease moves with fearsome rapidity and has taken the lives of 55 percent of those diagnosed. The mean average time between the appearance of symptoms and diagnosis is 3.5 months and the mean between diagnosis and death has held at 5.6 months. Some persons with AIDS (PWA) die within days of diagnosis while others have survived two or three years.

Who Is Affected

The catastrophic effects of AIDS primarily touches the lives of younger homosexual or bisexual males for the most part. Of the 20,760 cases cited, 47 percent are between 30-39 years old. Twenty-one percent are between 20-29 years old and another 21 percent are between 40-49 years of age. In the face of the ever-growing spread of this illness, it is necessary to know how the disease is transmitted and who are at risk for AIDS.

AIDS:HTLV disease is not spread because of who you are but what you do. It is spread by sexual acts involving the exchange of body fluids. The virus can also be spread through transfusion of untested blood (now all blood drawn in the United States is automatically tested), blood products, or the sharing of blood-contaminated needles. An infected mother can pass the virus to her newborn child before or during birth. It is not that a person is an

IV drug user that puts him at high risk for AIDS but that he shares his needle after usage with another. It is not a man's homosexual orientation that puts him at risk for AIDS. It is the kind of intimate behavior he might engage in that puts him at risk.

The disease is also financially devastating. From the onset of symptoms to death, the disease costs — out to $139,000.00 per case. Few in this age group have the capital or insurance coverage to underwrite their medical treatment. Hospital specialists are aware that AIDS is not only killing people — it is killing hospitals.

The Stigma

It is important to mention a corollary to our discussion of those at high risk. This is the factor of "stigma." Grievous illness isolates the sufferer. The AIDS patient experiences this isolation in a heightened manner due to the stigma which has been attached to this disease. A lack of understanding causes many to feel that the AIDS patient is a medical danger to them. In reality the man with the flu is more a danger to the AIDS patient than the PWA (person with AIDS) is to him. Then there are those who attach a religious significance to a person's diagnosis: "God is punishing you for your sexual orientation." Others through ignorance attach a moral judgment, thinking this is a disease of promiscuity while little realizing that it can be contracted from a single encounter.

The ignorance and judgments which stigmatize the AIDS patient then can be disastrous. Such ignorance has led to untold suffering in pediatric PWAs wherein young children are barred from classes and association with their playmates. Over 1,700 cases have been studied of those living with a diagnosed person with AIDS and in no cases has there been transmission of the virus through casual contact from the sufferer to the companion/care-giver. Nonetheless due to a widespread ignorance, a greater majority of PWAs can tell horror stories of being shunned, outcast and bereft of society.

A recently diagnosed PWA stated, "I wish I could tell my boss I had lung cancer . . . It would be so much easier." Another PWA rejoiced when his physician told him that along with his other infections, he now had lung cancer. He was almost elated and certainly relieved that now he could tell his mother that he was dying of a more respectable disease. He did not want her to suffer from his stigma. This is another factor of the AIDS stigma — it is multidirectional: you need not have AIDS to suffer from it. Support groups exist for families and friends of PWAs not only to help them cope with the death and dying of a child, friend, spouse, or brother but also to assist them in the area of stigma. The stigma surrounding AIDS has led some employers to terminate PWAs who were otherwise able to work. The AIDS stigma with its accompanying hysteria has led some to evict PWAs who have to seek refuge on the street and the public shelters. Too many PWAs can tell the litany of "man's inhumanity to man."

An Orthodox Response

For the early Church, the sick were always a special concern of the Christian community. Traditionally, when people fled to the countryside to avoid sickness, plagues, cholera and leprosy, the Church, composed of countless religious and lay persons, ministered to the sick and the dying in adherence to Saint Iakovos' admonition in his Epistle (read during every sacrament of Holy Unction): "Is anyone among you sick? Let him bring the presbyters of the Church, and let them pray over him, anointing him with oil in the name of the Lord" (Jas 1.14). Many of the ascetic Fathers of the Church dedicated their lives to serving lepers and other sick persons, and many of them fell victim to the same disease. Today, the Christian community is called to witness to the presence of Christ in those suffering from Acquired Immune Deficiency Syndrome (AIDS). Although the chances of catching AIDS are miniscule, the struggle against ignorance, superstition, and fear is the same as in the past. When the first federal government report on AIDS came out in June of 1981 by the Center for Disease Control in Atlanta, Georgia, very little was known about the disease. A few doctors have recognized a pattern of infectious diseases among homosexuals. After the first study, doctors from around the country began reporting similar cases. Most were homosexual men, although in Africa (where it is probably transmitted by prostitutes) it is just as common among heterosexuals.

Today, the most recent report tells us that intravenous drug users and blood transfusion recipients are also victims to this dread disease. From statistical research, about 6,000 Americans have died of AIDS and another 6,000 are known to have the disease. No one has recovered as yet. In New York City, AIDS is now the leading cause of death among men between 25 and 44 years of age. Some experts believe the number of AIDS patients will double by next summer. In addition, the Center for Disease Control believes that there are as many as 120,000 cases of AIDS-related complex or A.R.C., which does not always develop into AIDS. Finally, some studies estimate that there may be one million Americans who are symptomless carriers of the virus.

A few things about AIDS have become clear in the last four years. The disease is transmitted through the exchange of bodily fluids — primarily through sexual activity but also through the sharing of unsterilized hypodermic needles and through blood transfusions. Whether AIDS could be transmitted through saliva is as yet undetermined but considered unlikely. Testing procedures are now in place to eliminate blood transfusions as a cause of AIDS. It is also noteworthy that no doctors or nurses treating AIDS victims have died of the disease. If the disease were easily caught, medical personnel would be the first victims. No vaccine or cure is on the horizon, and much more private and government research is needed.

Recently, many clergymen of every denomination have contended that the AIDS victims are being punished for their sins. This is not only an ignorant point of view, it is also un-Orthodox. Although there is a relationship between sickness and man's sinful condition, we cannot consider sickness as a punishment which man suffers for his personal sins. In the sacrament of Holy Unction, at the prayer of anointing, the priest or bishop prays at the very end of the service: "O Holy Father, physician of souls and bodies, who did send Your only-begotten Son, our Lord Jesus Christ, who heals every infirmity and delivers us from death: heal also Your servants from the ills of the body and soul which do hinder them, and quicken them by the grace of Your Christ." And in the Gospel of John 9.3, we read: "Jesus answered, 'His blindness has nothing to do with his sins or his parents' sins. He is blind so that God's power might be seen at work in him.'" We must never stray from the true purpose of Christianity! We must see in the AIDS victim a brother or sister in Christ who deserves our love and our help. To use the Gospel or the Church to avoid our obligation to an AIDS victim is to shun Christ himself.

Christian hospitals, Orthodox physicians, chaplains, doctors, nurses, and other medical personnel have a special responsibility for the care of AIDS victims. It is, however, clear that the government is going to have to take a greater role in researching this disease and caring for its victims. But while love and compassion are offered to those stricken by AIDS, no one should falsely promise quick solutions that would lead people to doubt that monogamy and self-control not only make moral sense but medical sense as well.

The OCAMPR Report on AIDS

FORUM ON AIDS*

IN RESPONSE TO THE FIRST NATIONAL CONFERENCE PRESENtation on AIDS and because of concerns Orthodox Christians have expressed about the impact that the disease AIDS has had upon their lives and questions regarding the transmission of HIV, the Orthodox Christian Association of Medicine, Psychology and Religion convened a forum of leaders in these fields. This forum addressed specific questions raised by church leaders in an effort to offer interdisciplinary perspective relative to the faith and AIDS: 1) Should there be an alteration in the administration of Holy Communion to guard against contamination or in response to the fear of HIV? 2) Should people wanting to marry be tested for HIV? 3) What kind of behavior ought to be recommended in order to avoid the spread of AIDS? 4) How do we counsel people to respond to AIDS patients and to the fear of the spread of this disease?

This report is prepared to facilitate communication of Orthodox Christians about AIDS. It is not intended as a position paper as such but works to identify several points of view raised in the religious and scientific communities. This report is submitted with the hope that as the Church responds to the subject of AIDS, pastoral sensitivity will address the following concerns:

1. Should the administration of Holy Communion be altered from the *lavida* and chalice to guard against contamination or in response to the fear of HIV?

   A. Risk of Transmission of HIV and Holy Communion

---

*See forum members on p. 81.

Report on AIDS

Transmission of AIDS by Holy Communion seems to be highly unlikely, given the concentration of HIV at issue and the fragility of the virus. Current medical information, however, does not rule out transmission by way of the chalice.

AIDS has polarized some members within the Church body about the current practice for administering Holy Commmunion with reference to the potential of contamination of HIV vis-a-vis Holy Communion. On the one hand, Holy Communion is, for Orthodox Christians, the Body and Blood of Christ and thereby the vehicle for life, not death. On the other hand, the specific question raised by the disease of AIDS is whether the HIV virus, or germs generally, can be transmitted when one receives Holy Communion. Therefore, concern about AIDS has raised the wider question about transmission of germs generally via the current medium for receiving the communion.

Distinctions need to be drawn in this discussion. As faithful, Orthodox Christians affirm the reality of Jesus Christ in Holy Communion. At the same time it is noted that the purpose of Holy Communion is not understood as the means to lame destructive viruses, but as the Body and Blood of Christ, Holy Communion works to heal according to one's faith and to the Grace of God. Therefore, one cannot be certain about the impact of agents such as germs or HIV in Holy Communion neutralizes a virus or germ.

This has brought receiving Holy Communion for some to the plateau of being a test to evaluate one's spiritual and possibly physical well-being. Holy Communion should not be perceived as a test for God or for the individual concerning his or her relationship with Him. As the current practice for the administration of receiving Holy Communion has created such a challenge for some of the members of the Church body, this subject invites a pastoral response.

B. Pastoral Concerns Regarding Altering the Form of Administration of Holy Communion

Church history indicates that there has been variation in the administration of Holy Communion. At the current time there is no agreement about the need or of concensus about the form for altering Holy Communion in the Church body, yet change should not be viewed as either inherently "good" or "bad". Change which is consistent with the Orthodox Tradition is conceivable within the Church. Therefore, as this matter is considered, change should not evolve as a response to fear but may occur as a legitimate expression of pastoral sensitivity.

Should people wanting to marry be tested for HIV?

Generally, if one has doubt whether or not he or she has been exposed to HIV, it is advisable for that person to be tested for HIV antibodies. It is important for potential spouses to know whether they carriers of HIV or if they are at risk of contracting AIDS after marriage. In the interest of facilitating and supporting a solid base for a prospective marriage in these days, AIDS testing before marriage would probably be reassuring to a couple and would be possibly helpful; so it is recommended.

At the same time, it is noted that test results have various limitations. The Church should be supportive and encourage such practices but should not be involved in technical, procedural or legal aspects or requirements for such testing before marriage.

3. What kind of behavior ought to be recommended in order to avoid the spread of AIDS?

By being informed about the disease and its spread, behaviors which are in accordance with the faith (e. g., morality against promiscuity, prostitution, drug abuse) and which avoid routes for the spread of the disease dangers (e. g., needle sharing) need to be encouraged. In the scientific community, monogamous behavior is recommended to avoid or at least to decrease the spread of AIDS.

Sexual education in the Church is supported which would encourage dating with awareness of one's behavior, chastity and perhaps "pre-intimate" testing for HIV antibodies. Religious education that addresses these concerns should explore guidance of the faithful toward lifetime, monogamous relationships based upon trust, love and fidelity.

4. How do you counsel people to respond to AIDS patients and to the fear of the spread of this disease?

The faithful should be educated as to the means of contracting HIV. Family studies about the absence of the spread of HIV from thousands of AIDS patients from non-sexual, close and familial contacts strongly supports that HIV does not spread via close personal contact. As people feel less at risk by such interaction and through education, social attitudes will improve.

Compassion of the faithful for those who are affected by the illness and their families needs to be encouraged. The Church must actively work against prejudice and fear through its spiritual resources of Christian hope, faith and love and through specific educational efforts.

Sexual education concerning one's faith generally should be part of religious programming. Subjects such as multiple sexual encounters, sexual expression, monogamy and abstinence, as well as the subject of drugs, need to be addressed openly, directly and in the tradition of the faith. Additionally, the counsel of the faith regarding the responses of love, compassion and death are essential to apply when considering eduaction about AIDS and an Orthodox Christian response.

The subject of AIDS is one the most critical problems of this century. The Church has a responsibility to provide leadership, direction and counsel regarding various aspects of this issue and to draw upon the resourcefulness of the Body of Believers with the guidance of Jesus Christ in its response.

FORUM

Dr. George Canellos — Professor of Medicine, Harvard Medical School; Medical Director, Dana Farber Cancer Institute.

Dr. John Chirban (Chairman) — Professor of Psychology, Hellenic College; Associate in Human Development, Harvard University.

Rev. Dr. Stanley Harakas — Professor of Orthodox Theology and Christian Ethics, Holy Cross School of Theology.

Dr. Matina S. Horner — President, Radcliffe College; Associate Professor of Psychology, Harvard University.

Rev. George Johnson — Pastor, Johnstown, Pennsylvania, Orthodox Church in America.

Dr. Nikos Kakaviatos — Cardiologist; President, Washington, D.C. District OCAMPR.

Rev. Dr. Gerard Machado — Chairman, Department of Psychology The Veteran's Hospital, New Jersey; Mission Priest, Orthodox Church in America.

His Grace Bishop Methodios of Boston — President, Hellenic College/Holy Cross Greek Orthodox School of Theology.

Dr. Anthony Parris — Dermatologist; Chairman, OCAMPR Division of Medicine.

Dr. George Pazin — Infectious Disease Specialist, Professor of Medicine, University of Pittsburgh.

Mr. Peter Poulos — Director of Clinical Pastoral Education, The Methodist Hospital, Brooklyn, New York.

Rev. Dr. Theodore Stylianopoulos — Professor of New Testament and Orthodox Spirituality, Holy Cross Greek Orthodox School of Theology.

CONTRIBUTORS

John Breck, Ph.D. is Associate Professor of Ethics and New Testament at St. Vladimir's Seminary and Associate Editor of *St. Vladimir's Quarterly.* Fr. John Breck was the first district coordinator for the New York O.C.A.M.P.R.

John T. Chirban, Ph.D., Th.D. is Professor of Psychology and Co-Director of Counseling and Spiritual Development at Hellenic College and Holy Cross School of Theology. He is the founder and president of the O.C.A.M.P.R.

John Demakis, M.D. is Associate Professor of Medicine at Loyola University Stritch School of Medicine, Maywood, Illinois. Dr. Demakis is the district coordinator for the Chicago O.C.A.M.P.R. and coordinator for the O.C.A.M.P.R. missions efforts.

Peter Diamandis, M.D. is founder and president of the International Space University.

Milton B. Efthimiou, Ph.D. is Director of the Office of Social Concerns for the Greek Orthodox Archdiocese.

Nicholas Kokonis, Ph.D. is a psychologist in private practice affiliated with the Swedish Covenant Hospital, Chicago, Illinois. He was the chairman of the Second National O.C.A.M.P.R. Conference.

Nicholas Krommydas, Th.D. (candidate) is chancellor of the Greek Orthodox Diocese of Boston, instructor in pastoral counseling, and Co-Director of Counseling and Spiritual Development. Fr. Krommydas is the coordinator for Religion for the O.C.A.M.P.R.

John Meyendorff, Ph.D. is Dean and Professor of Church History at St. Vladimir's Seminary and editor of *St. Vladimir's Quarterly.*

George Pazin, M.D. is Associate Professor of Medicine at the University of Pittsburgh School of Medicine and serves on the National Board of Infectious Disease and Acquired Immune Deficiency Syndrome.

Peter Poulos, Th.M., C.S.W. is Director of Training in the Department of Pastoral Care at the Methodist Hospital, Brooklyn, New York.

Theoharis C. Theoharides, Ph.D., M.D. is Associate Professor of Biochemistry, Pharmacology and Psychiatry and Director of Medical Pharmacology, Tufts School of Medicine, Boston, Massachusetts.